ADVISER

ERIC H. CLINE, Department of Classical and Near Eastern Languages and Civilizations, professor of classics and of anthropology, George Washington University

THE WORLD OF THE BIBLE

BIBLICAL STORIES AND THE ARCHAEOLOGY BEHIND THEM

JILL RUBALCABA

FOREWORD BY JEAN-PIERRE ISBOUTS

NATIONAL GEOGRAPHIC

WASHINGTON, D.C.

TABLE OF CONTENTS

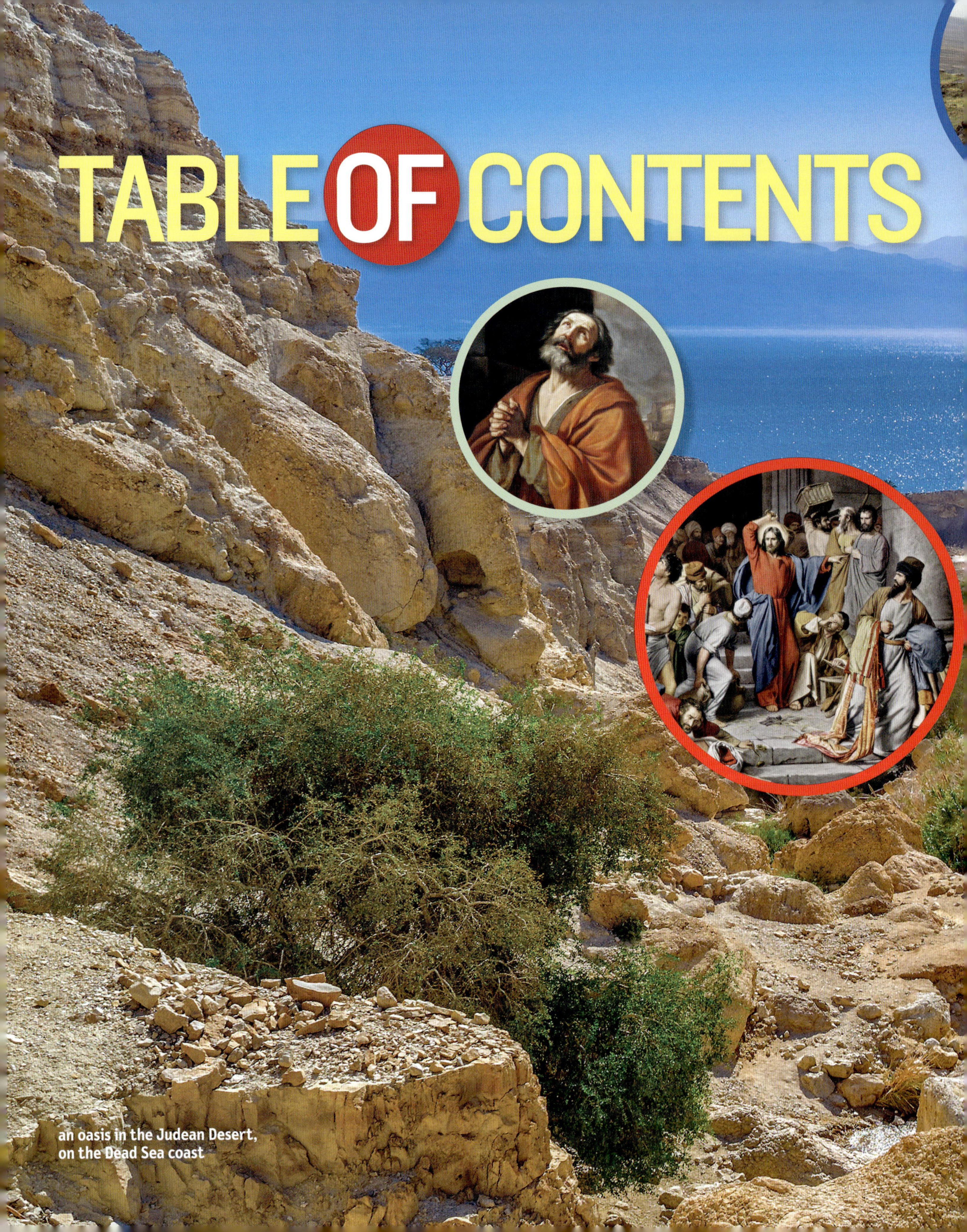

an oasis in the Judean Desert, on the Dead Sea coast

"The Conversion of St. Paul," by Marco da Siena, 1545, in the church of Santo Spirito in Sassia, in Rome, Italy

Why is the Bible such an important book? That is a question that many people have asked over the centuries. After all, the stories in the Bible were written many hundreds, even thousands, of years ago. Why should it matter to us today?

One answer is that for Jews and Christians, the Bible is the word of God. In other words, for them the stories and ideas of the Bible were actually *inspired* by God.

But there is also another reason to get to know the Bible. The Bible is not just one book: It is a collection of books, each written in a different place and time. That is reflected in the word "bible" itself, which is an English translation of the Greek word *biblia,* meaning "many books." The oldest of these books have stories that go back nearly 4,000 years, to the time of ancient Mesopotamia and Babylon. Others, such as the story of Joseph, are set in ancient Egypt, while the two Books of Kings took shape when much of the Middle East was ruled by ancient Assyria, and later, the Persian and Greek Empires.

The first thing you see when you pick up a Bible is that it is organized into two major parts. The first part is the Hebrew Bible, which Christians call the Old Testament. These are the sacred writings, or scripture, of the Jewish people across the 1,000-year history of ancient Israel. This part of the Bible begins with God's creation of the world and continues with the fascinating adventures of people who enjoyed God's special protection: from Noah to Abraham, from Jacob to Joseph, and from Moses to Joshua. We can also find wonderful poetry and songs in the Bible, in books like the Psalms or Proverbs. So the Hebrew Bible, the Old Testament, is not just one story: It's an amazing collection of 39 different books that each tells us about the many ways in which we can enjoy and understand the meaning of life.

The second part is the New Testament. This is the sacred scripture of Christians. It contains 27 books, beginning with the four Gospels of Matthew, Mark, Luke, and John, written in Greek. The word "gospel" is actually derived from an old English word named "goodspell" or "good news," a translation of the Greek word *euangelion.* That good news celebrates the coming of Jesus as the savior of humankind. But the Gospels are not like modern biographies about famous people that we read today. Instead, they focus on the last two or three years of Jesus' life on Earth, which he spent ministering to the people of Galilee and Judea. They tell us about his teachings and wondrous deeds and show why Jesus was the Messiah, and the Son of God.

Together, the Hebrew and Christian Bibles tell us so much about how we can live our lives as loving and responsible people. They are truly a compass by which we can chart a course through the complexities of modern life. That is why *The World of the Bible* is such an important book. It is a wonderful introduction to the most important stories in the Bible in a way that's both entertaining and inspiring. And it will also tell you about some of the amazing discoveries that archaeologists have made in recent decades, which help us to imagine what life in biblical times was really like. In sum, *The World of the Bible* is an invaluable guide that every family will enjoy.

JEAN-PIERRE ISBOUTS

Author of National Geographic's *The Biblical World* and *Archaeology of the Bible*

PUBLISHER'S NOTE

In this book, you'll find specific passages, or lines of text, that appear in the Bible as well as facts about things that happened during biblical times. As you turn the pages, you'll notice two kinds of spreads. Some spreads are Bible stories, which may be familiar or not. Other spreads are about discoveries in history and archaeology that tell us more about the people and places in the Bible stories. The Bible passages for the stories are annotated at the top of each story's page. Each annotation lists the name of the book in the Bible from which it came; the chapter, or section of the book; and the verse, or specific lines in the chapter. For instance, on page 20 the excerpt is from Genesis 11:1–9—that is, the Book of Genesis, chapter 11, verses 1–9.

The translation of the Bible used to compile the content in this book is the New Revised Standard Version of the Bible (NRSV). We hope you'll enjoy these stories about the biblical world.

STORIES AND DISCOVERIES

Stories from the Bible tell us about early civilization in Asia, across northern Africa, and into Europe. Gardens, deserts, towns, and bodies of water are settings for these stories. Archaeologists are learning how the stories may be true and what other discoveries they can make about the people and events in those ancient places. The blue boxes below are Bible stories; the green boxes tell about true discoveries in these places today.

MISSIONARY

Once an enemy of Christians, Paul later traveled from Antioch across Europe to spread Christian teachings. (pages 118–119)

THE CATACOMBS

Early Christians dug a maze of tunnels beneath the city of Rome to use as secret meeting places and to bury their dead. (pages 120–121)

TRADERS OF THE SEA

Seafaring traders called Phoenicians carried timber from Tyre to Jerusalem to build Solomon's Temple; they also traded along the Mediterranean coast. (pages 42–43)

BABY MOSES

The pharaoh's daughter found a Hebrew baby hidden in the bulrushes of the Nile. She named him Moses. (pages 44–45)

THE TEN COMMANDMENTS

After the Israelites escaped Egypt, God presented Moses with the Ten Commandments on Mount Sinai. (pages 54–55)

MAP KEY

- Archaeological discoveries
- Stories from the Bible
- Place associated with Jesus
- • Other cities of the Biblical world

FROM THE BIBLICAL WORLD: 20TH CENTURY B.C.E. TO 1ST CENTURY C.E.

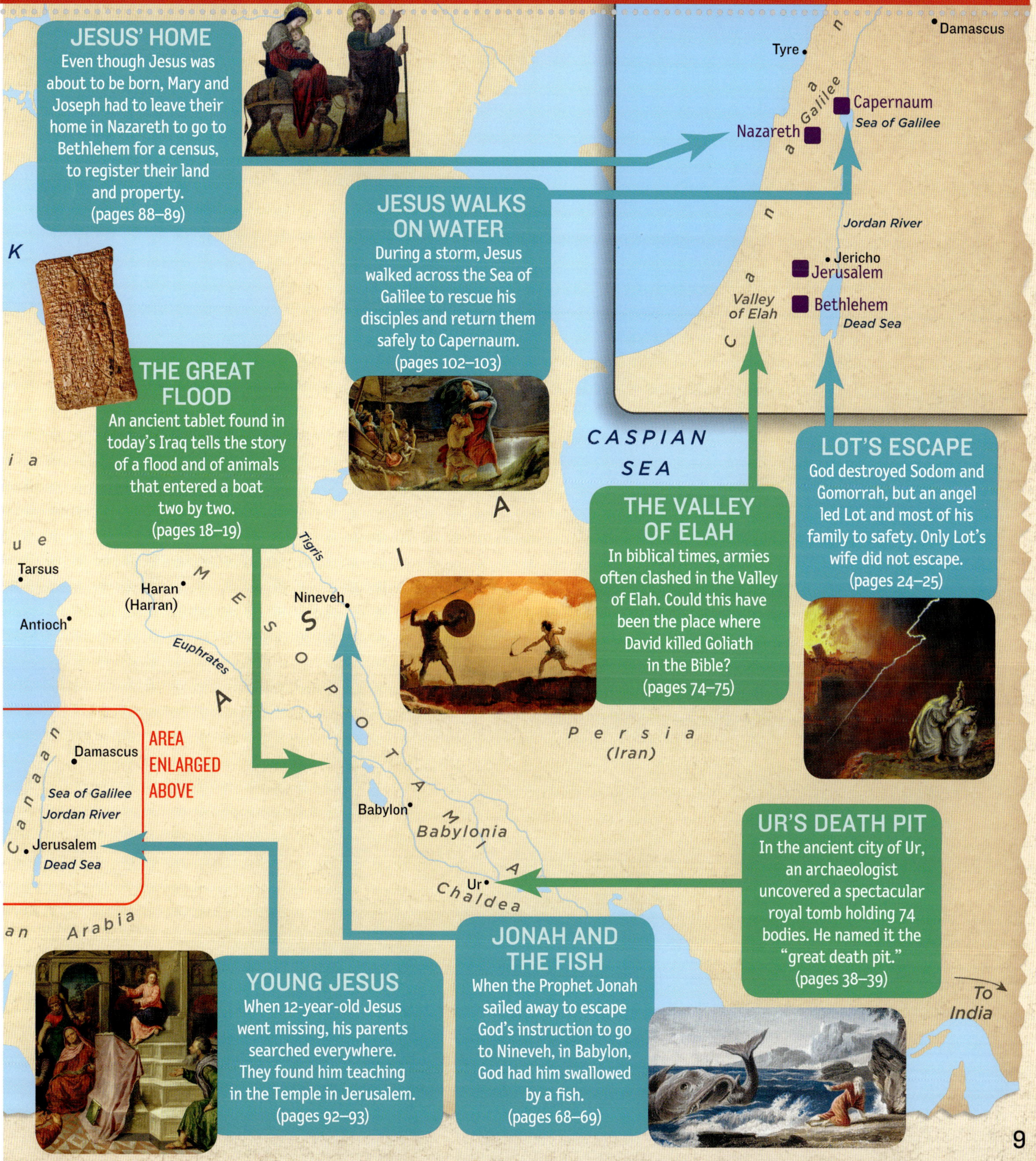

JESUS' HOME

Even though Jesus was about to be born, Mary and Joseph had to leave their home in Nazareth to go to Bethlehem for a census, to register their land and property.
(pages 88–89)

JESUS WALKS ON WATER

During a storm, Jesus walked across the Sea of Galilee to rescue his disciples and return them safely to Capernaum.
(pages 102–103)

THE GREAT FLOOD

An ancient tablet found in today's Iraq tells the story of a flood and of animals that entered a boat two by two.
(pages 18–19)

THE VALLEY OF ELAH

In biblical times, armies often clashed in the Valley of Elah. Could this have been the place where David killed Goliath in the Bible?
(pages 74–75)

LOT'S ESCAPE

God destroyed Sodom and Gomorrah, but an angel led Lot and most of his family to safety. Only Lot's wife did not escape.
(pages 24–25)

UR'S DEATH PIT

In the ancient city of Ur, an archaeologist uncovered a spectacular royal tomb holding 74 bodies. He named it the "great death pit."
(pages 38–39)

YOUNG JESUS

When 12-year-old Jesus went missing, his parents searched everywhere. They found him teaching in the Temple in Jerusalem.
(pages 92–93)

JONAH AND THE FISH

When the Prophet Jonah sailed away to escape God's instruction to go to Nineveh, in Babylon, God had him swallowed by a fish.
(pages 68–69)

PART I OLD TESTAMENT: STORIES AND DISCOVERIES

The Old Testament is much more than a collection of stories about the beginning of humankind and the experiences of an ancient people. It is more than a look at life in ancient Mesopotamia, an area in the Middle East between the great Tigris and Euphrates Rivers. It is a collection of books that contain poetry and songs, laws and wisdom, and hundreds of stories about God's relationship with people. Together, these writings tell about families, rulers, battles, worship, and the Israelites' long migration to the Promised Land.

On the following pages, you will encounter two different kinds of spreads: You will read stories that are retellings of biblical verse, such as the one about Adam and Eve in the Garden of Eden. On other pages you will discover how archaeologists in the field today are trying to reconstruct the history of the Old Testament's people and places through the artifacts they left behind. You will be amazed by reading about a variety of Bible topics, such as Noah and his ark and the buildings of the biblical world. As you read, you will begin to see that the people and places of the biblical world are in many ways similar to those of today's world.

"Thus the **heavens** and the **earth** were finished, and all their multitude. And on the seventh day **GOD FINISHED THE WORK** that he had done and he **RESTED.**"

—GENESIS 2:1–2

"The Creation of the Birds and Fishes," by Isaak van Oosten, 17th century C.E.

GENESIS 2–3

THE STORY OF ADAM AND EVE

After God made the Earth and filled it with plants and animals, God made humankind.

From dust God molded the body of a man, then gave him life. He placed the naked man, Adam, in a magnificent garden called Eden. In the center of Eden, he planted the tree of life and the tree of knowledge.

God told Adam that he could eat from every tree—except the tree of knowledge.

God decided Adam needed a partner, and so he put Adam into a deep sleep, and took one of Adam's ribs. From that rib, God made Eve, also naked.

One day a sly serpent asked Eve, "Did God forbid you to eat anything?"

"There is only one forbidden tree," she answered. "The tree of knowledge."

The serpent whispered, "God doesn't want you to have knowledge."

Eve thought, "If the tree has the power to make me wise, how can I not eat from it?"

After taking a bite, she offered the fruit to Adam. He took a bite, too. Suddenly, they were embarrassed of their nakedness. They quickly covered themselves with fig leaves. Then they hid.

That evening God called for Adam. Adam cried out from his hiding place: "I heard you call, but I was afraid because I'm naked."

"How did you know you were naked?" God asked. "You must have eaten from the tree of knowledge!"

"It was Eve," Adam said. "She gave me the fruit."

"The serpent tricked me," Eve said.

God pointed at the serpent. "You will crawl on your belly and eat dust forevermore."

Then God turned to Eve. "Giving birth will bring terrible pain."

Lastly, he cursed Adam. "You were made from dust, and in death you will return to dust."

With that, God cast Adam and Eve out of Eden.

DID YOU KNOW?

Stories throughout history tell how **TREES BEARING THE GIFTS OF LIFE AND KNOWLEDGE NEEDED GUARDING.** In the Hebrew Bible, an angel disguised as a fiery serpent called **A SERAPH** wields a blazing sword to protect the tree of life. The Greek mythological hero Hercules has to slay **A DRAGON** with 100 heads that guards the apple tree of knowledge. In Persian mythology, **A PAIR OF FISH** protect the tree of life in a staring contest with an **EVIL FROG.**

"Adam and Eve in the Garden of Eden," by Wenzel Peter, 19th century C.E.

WHERE IS PARADISE?

Eden hasn't been found yet. The stories in the Book of Genesis take place before writing was invented, so there are no true written records. There are no helpful ancient road signs saying "Entering Eden" either. But experts are looking for clues to this paradise. The Bible describes a river flowing out of Eden that branches into four rivers—the Pishon, Gihon, Tigris, and Euphrates. Of the four rivers only two—the Euphrates and the Tigris—have the same names today. But are they the same rivers? And do they follow the same path they did in ancient times? And where are the Pishon and the Gihon? Archaeogeologists (scientists who study the Earth's formations of the ancient past) attempt to answer these questions.

Archaeogeologists carefully go through satellite images looking for fossil rivers—rivers that dried up long ago. By studying these images, they can see how the moving water gradually cut away the riverbeds—just as the Colorado River cuts through the Grand Canyon, but not as deep. Using data from the images, some scientists think that Eden could now be underwater in today's Persian Gulf where the Tigris and Euphrates once came together. In ancient times, the Persian Gulf was dry land in southern Mesopotamia.

Other scientists think the nearby Arabian Peninsula is a more likely location for Eden because they identified a fossil river that could have been the Pishon. But neither location is certain.

detail from a 12th-century C.E. Catalan fresco depicting Adam and Eve

One of the challenges of using today's maps is that most rivers flow the opposite way of how the Bible describes them flowing! Today smaller streams and tributaries feed into larger rivers. The Bible says that the larger rivers flowed into smaller streams and tributaries. The height of the land changed over time, and this likely changed the flow of the rivers.

The Bible says that all plants and animals thrived in Eden, and Eden is where Adam named them all. Archaeobotanists (scientists who study ancient plants) and archaeozoologists (scientists who study ancient animals) have determined that an area called the Fertile Crescent is where plants and animals were first tamed by humans.

The Fertile Crescent is a huge area shaped like a crescent moon. It contains all of what was Mesopotamia. That includes today's Mediterranean coast, Syria, Jordan, Israel, Palestine, Lebanon, Iraq, Kuwait, Cyprus, and parts of Iraq, Egypt, Turkey, and more. The area also contains the Tigris and Euphrates Rivers and the fertile land around them. Because the Bible says these two rivers were in Eden, this could have been the place: a lush oasis, surrounded by desert.

Scientists haven't had much luck finding the exact location yet. But they continue to search.

THE NAME ADAM COMES FROM THE HEBREW WORD ADAMA, meaning "EARTH."

palm trees in
a tropical garden

DID YOU KNOW?

TRADITION over the past several centuries says that **MOUNT ARARAT** in today's Turkey was the final resting place for **NOAH'S ARK** after the floodwaters receded. **TODAY** the ark is an important symbol for citizens of **ARMENIA,** which borders Turkey, and **THE ARK EVEN APPEARS ON THEIR FLAG.**

"Noah's Ark on the Mount Ararat," by Simon de Myle, about 1570 C.E.

GENESIS 6–8

NOAH AND THE FLOOD

God regretted creating humans. Humans were corrupt in their hearts and violent in their deeds. God decided to clean the slate and begin again. Only one human pleased God. His name was Noah.

God spoke to Noah: "You must build an ark from cypress. Cover it inside and out with tarlike pitch. Make three levels, with a door in the side, and a roof overhead." God told Noah exactly how big the ark should be.

God planned to flood the Earth. He promised to save Noah and his family, but first Noah had to collect one pair of every creature—one male and one female, including things that flew and things that crept.

Once Noah finished the ark and the people and creatures were safely inside, God sealed them in. It started to rain. Fountains of water burst from the ground, and rain poured from the sky.

For 40 days and 40 nights the rain drummed on the ark's roof. The water rose so high it covered the mountains.

One morning a wind picked up and the rain stopped. Gradually, the water level fell and the ark settled on "the mountains of Ararat," which experts think refers to an area in Iran, not to the actual Mount Ararat in Turkey. Noah opened a window but saw only water in every direction.

Noah sent a raven and then a dove to find dry land. They both flew back.

A week later Noah sent the dove out again. When it returned, it held an olive leaf in its beak.

The following week he sent the dove out once more—this time it did not come back. It must have found a place to roost. Noah and his family removed the roof and saw that the Earth was no longer covered in water. It took more than a year for the Earth to become completely dry again.

At last God told Noah that it was time to leave the ark along with all the animals—to go forth and multiply.

Coracles have been used for centuries in biblical lands.

THE ARK TABLET

Flood stories like the story of Noah in the Bible's Book of Genesis are common in the literature of ancient cultures. Scientists have found them in Mesopotamia, Syria, Egypt, Europe, Greece, India, New Guinea, Australia, and in Central, North, and South America. Stories of floods that destroy a world gone bad appear in Sumerian and Mesopotamian mythology dating back thousands of years. In the stories, there is one hero who survives by building a boat. One of the most well-known and earliest mentions of a great flood comes from *The Epic of Gilgamesh*, a Mesopotamian poem written sometime around 2100 B.C.E.

At the British Museum in London, curator Irving Finkel, an expert in ancient Assyrian culture, studied a similar story on what is now known as the Ark Tablet. Nearly 4,000 years old, the Ark Tablet is a clay tablet from Mesopotamia. It is small enough to hold in your hand—smaller than a paperback book. On it, 60 lines are written in cuneiform, the oldest known form of writing used in the Middle East, from around 3200 B.C.E. to 200 C.E. Cuneiform consists of a series of wedgelike symbols made with wedge-shaped instruments, often reeds. The symbols are arranged in different patterns for different meanings.

Words inscribed into the ancient Ark Tablet tell the story of building a huge ark.

The Ark Tablet tells the story of a Mesopotamian god, Enki, who gave instructions to a Noah-like hero, Atrahasis, to build a round lifeboat. "Draw out the boat that you will make, on a circular plan," Enki told Atrahasis. The ark Enki described was enormous, nearly the size of a football field. Unlike Noah's ark, which the Bible says was constructed with cypress wood, Atrahasis was to make his ark with rope. He was to coil the rope again and again into a bowl-shaped basket. In the Ark Tablet, lines 15 to 16 describe how Atrahasis was to use J-shaped ribs made of wood to support the 20-foot (6-m)-high rope walls. These supports also allowed him to build a roof, an upper deck, and stalls for housing animals. To make the boat waterproof, Enki advised Atrahasis to use bitumen, a tarry substance that bubbled up from the ground in Mesopotamia. He would caulk, or fill, the boat's seams and crevices to make them watertight and keep the boat afloat. Twenty of the tablet's 60 lines give directions on how to caulk the ark inside and out.

Irving Finkel had spent a lifetime deciphering tablets. But lines 51 and 52 of the Ark Tablet shocked him. To read them, he polished his magnifying glass and tipped the tablet this way and that under a bright light. Squinting his eyes just so, he was able to make out the wording: "and the wild animals." What came next was even more startling. Line 52 begins with the characters "sa" and "na." Finkel searched for their meaning in the Chicago Assyrian Dictionary. To his astonishment, he discovered that together they made "sana"—a very rare word that meant "two by two."

It was now evident that this ancient Mesopotamian flood story was much closer to the biblical version than anyone had suspected, not only with a Noah-like character and a giant ark but also with animals boarding two by two.

Round boats called CORACLES are still common around the world. They sit **on top of the water rather** than in it. Most are small **one-person vessels** propelled by a single oar.

GENESIS 11:1–9

THE TOWER OF BABEL

After the Flood, Noah's family left the ark and followed God's command to "be fruitful and multiply." Noah's three sons moved in different directions and became the founders of great nations. Despite living far apart, all the nations spoke the same language. This bond of common language made them feel as though they could accomplish anything.

Some of the family members began building a town with sturdy mud bricks they had baked. As the town grew, so did their ambition. They decided to build a tower so tall it reached the heavens. They named their town Babel, which meant "gate of the gods" in Akkadian—the earliest language spoken in Mesopotamia—and set about to build their soaring tower.

As God watched them, he realized the mortals had lost their way. Why were they so prideful, trying to ascend to the heavens instead of prospering on Earth, as he had commanded? What vanity made them think they had a right to make their way to his realm?

God decided to teach them a lesson. The very thing that brought these people together also made them conceited—their language. If they couldn't understand one another, they couldn't work together and the tower building would stop.

God gave them different languages. So when they spoke to one another, the words made no sense and they were all confused. It was as if they all were babbling. They stopped building the tower and the city, and they scattered all over the Earth.

The town's name, Babel, is close to the Hebrew word for "confusion."

DID YOU KNOW?

The **INSPIRATION** for the Tower of Babel story may have come from **ancient ziggurats,** which were immense temple complexes in Mesopotamia. These massive brick structures were most often square or rectangular and **TIERED LIKE A WEDDING CAKE,** with a temple or shrine at the top.

In the 1920s, archaeologist Leonard Woolley excavated the **4,000-YEAR-OLD GREAT ZIGGURAT OF UR.** It was built with heavy bricks weighing up to 33 pounds (15 kg) each. The base alone has 720,000 of them.

"The Tower of Babel," by Pieter Bruegel the Elder, 1563 C.E.

GENESIS 17, 21, 22

THE ULTIMATE SACRIFICE

Abraham was 100 years old when he finally had a son with his wife Sarah. For almost a century, he'd yearned for a child, and when God told him that Sarah, who was 90 years old, would soon bear him a son, he laughed. It seemed impossible. And yet Sarah gave birth to a boy. As God instructed, Abraham named his son Isaac, which means "he laughs" in ancient Hebrew.

Several years later, God spoke again to Abraham about his son. This time, it was to test Abraham's faith. "Abraham," God commanded, "take your beloved son, Isaac, and go to the land of Moriah, and sacrifice him there as a burnt offering."

Early the next morning, Abraham obediently prepared for the journey, telling Isaac only that they were going to make an offering to God. They cut wood for the offering, saddled their donkey, and set out.

After three days, they reached the foot of the mountain where he was to sacrifice Isaac.

Abraham had Isaac carry the wood. Abraham carried a knife and the fire.

"Father," asked Isaac, "where is the lamb for the sacrifice?"

"God will provide," Abraham answered, and they continued on.

When they reached the spot God had told him about, Abraham built a stone altar and piled wood on it. Then Abraham tied Isaac up and laid him on the woodpile. Abraham raised his knife.

"Abraham, Abraham!" an angel's voice from heaven cried out. "Stop."

The angel told Abraham he'd proved his commitment to God. He'd been willing to sacrifice his beloved son.

Just then, something in the bushes caught Abraham's attention. It was a lamb, whose horns were tangled in the branches. God had provided.

Abraham released Isaac and burned the lamb as an offering instead.

The angel told Abraham, "Because you were willing to sacrifice for God, you will be blessed. Your descendants will be as numerous as the stars in the sky."

As God had promised, Abraham became one of Israel's three great patriarchs—father to a great nation.

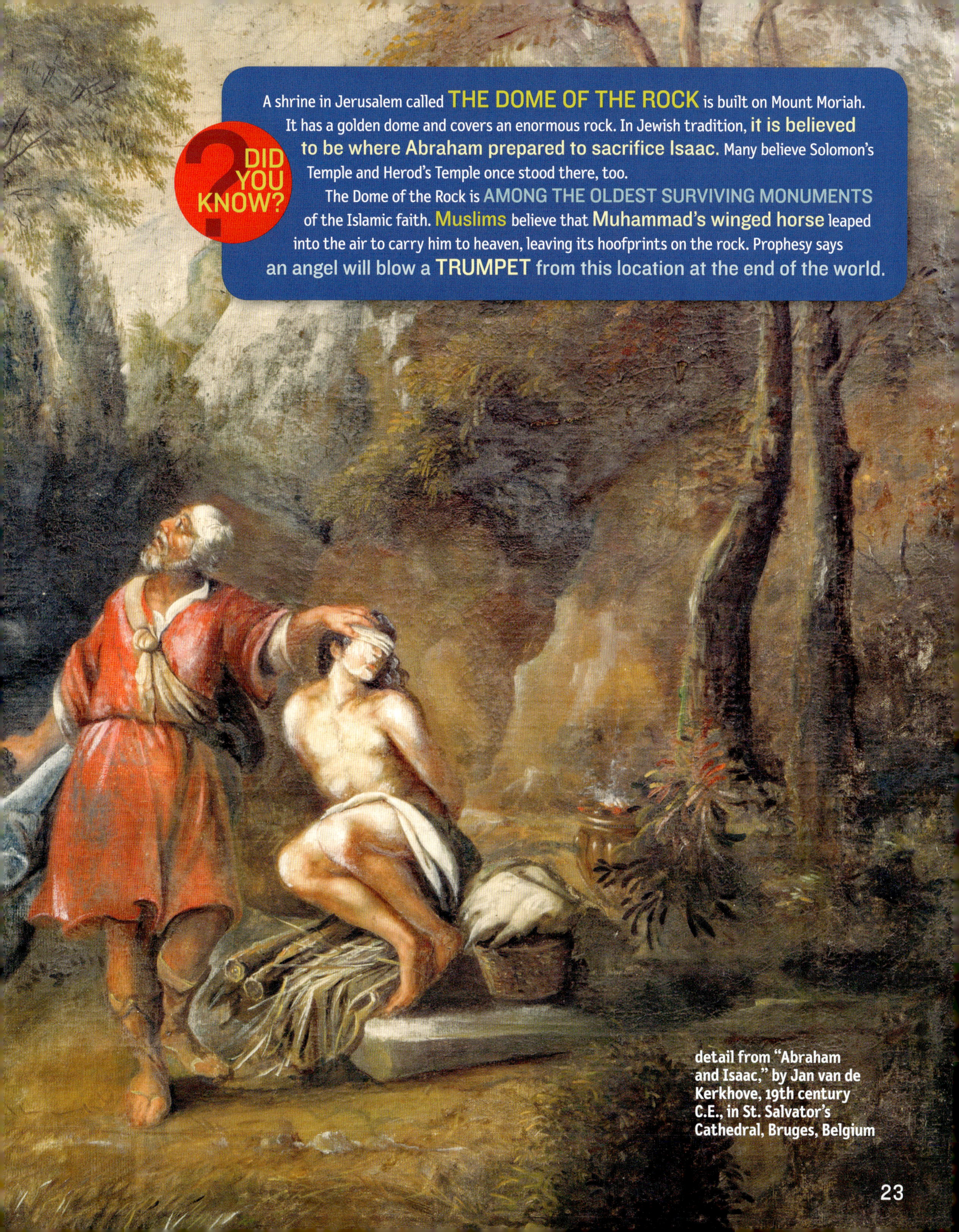

DID YOU KNOW?

A shrine in Jerusalem called **THE DOME OF THE ROCK** is built on Mount Moriah. It has a golden dome and covers an enormous rock. In Jewish tradition, **it is believed to be where Abraham prepared to sacrifice Isaac.** Many believe Solomon's Temple and Herod's Temple once stood there, too.

The Dome of the Rock is **AMONG THE OLDEST SURVIVING MONUMENTS** of the Islamic faith. **Muslims** believe that **Muhammad's winged horse** leaped into the air to carry him to heaven, leaving its hoofprints on the rock. Prophesy says **an angel will blow a TRUMPET from this location at the end of the world.**

detail from "Abraham and Isaac," by Jan van de Kerkhove, 19th century C.E., in St. Salvator's Cathedral, Bruges, Belgium

GENESIS 19

A TALE OF TWO CITIES

The two cities of Sodom and Gomorrah had a reputation for wickedness. God decided the cities must be destroyed. But God liked Abraham, and Abraham's nephew Lot lived in Sodom.

God sent two angels to Sodom to save Lot and his family. When the angels arrived, looking like ordinary men, Lot was sitting at the city gate. Lot invited the angels to his home for the night. After dinner, just as they were about to go to sleep, a mob gathered outside Lot's house. Lot went out to see what they wanted. They demanded to see the newcomers. When Lot refused, the mob threatened to break down Lot's door. Before anything bad could happen, the angels pulled Lot back inside. Then they struck the mob blind so the people couldn't find the door.

The angels told Lot it was time to gather his family and get out. God was about to destroy the city. There was no time to lose. But when Lot tried to get his sons-in-law to come with him, the young men thought Lot was kidding and refused to leave.

At daybreak, the angels told Lot it was now or never. "Get your wife and two daughters." When Lot didn't move fast enough, the angels grabbed him by the hand and pulled him and his wife and two daughters out the door.

"Run for your life," they told Lot. "Run to the hills. Don't stop. *Don't look back!*"

They ran. And while they ran, God filled the sky with fire and sulfur that rained down on the cities. Amid the chaos, Lot and his daughters kept running, but his wife looked back. With that one disobedient glance, she turned into a pillar of salt.

The following morning, all that could be seen on the plain where the cities of Sodom and Gomorrah once stood was thick, black smoke, rising like it was coming from a furnace. God's judgment on Sodom and Gomorrah had been fulfilled.

DID YOU KNOW?

While some experts have suggested that the archaeological sites **Bab edh-Dhra** and **Numeira** could have been the ancient cities of **Sodom and Gomorrah,** recent research shows that this is **NOT POSSIBLE** because they are not from the right time period. Still, the cities' stories are tragically similar.

A thick layer of **volcanic ash** at both Bab edh-Dhra and Numeira suggests that **A VOLCANIC ERUPTION BROUGHT A VIOLENT END TO THESE TWO CITIES thousands of years ago.** The bodies of three people at Numeira, trapped by a falling tower, indicate it may have been an **EARTHQUAKE** that caused the destruction of the area.

"The Destruction of Sodom and Gomorrah," by John Martin, 1852 C.E.

aerial photograph of
the southern basin
of the Dead Sea

FIRE AND BRIMSTONE

Many people have searched for the ancient cities of Sodom and Gomorrah over the years, but the Bible's Book of Genesis gives only a few clues about the location of these two "cities of the plain."

The Bible uses the Hebrew word *kikkar* for "plain" when it refers to the location of Sodom and Gomorrah. Because elsewhere in the Old Testament kikkar is used to describe flat circular objects such as metal disks called talents and round flat loaves of bread, some experts think the cities were in a round plain. If so, a good candidate would be the plain of the River Jordan, north of the Dead Sea.

The area around Sodom and Gomorrah was filled with bitumen pits—bubbling pits of a black tarry substance that the builders in Babel used to make mortar for their bricks. Geologists have found evidence of bitumen beneath the shallow southern basin of the Dead Sea, so it's possible that the cities were located there.

A pillar of rock salt at Mount Sodom, looking like a female figure, is called Lot's Wife.

The area south of the Dead Sea is also home to a salt and rock formation known as Lot's Wife. In an earthquake 4,000 years ago, the roof of a salt cave collapsed, leaving this supporting pillar shaped like a person. Could this sudden appearance of a pillar of salt amid the chaos and destruction of an earthquake be what led to the biblical story?

Scientists also speculate about what might have caused a rain of fire and sulfur as the Bible describes. One theory is that an earthquake forced natural gas up through cracks in the earth. A spark from a lamp or a cooking fire in the city could have ignited the gas, causing an explosion so forceful it propelled flaming minerals into the air. These fiery globs would then fall from the sky and smolder for days.

Another theory also involves an earthquake south of the Dead Sea where these tremors are common. In this scenario, after the earthquake the cities floated momentarily on a layer of groundwater. Suddenly, gravity pulled the cities into the sea, releasing pockets of natural gas that burst into flames. Could earthquakes have set off a chain reaction of explosions, chemical fires, and death?

A team of scientists intent on discovering whether or not an earthquake could cause the complete destruction described in the Bible built a model to scale. They constructed the type of buildings that would have been built nearly 4,500 years ago and used the exact type of ground the structures would have been built on. Spinning the model in a centrifuge—a machine that goes around and around—increased the gravity to the point where the models would behave like full-size buildings. The scientists then created the force of a magnitude 6 earthquake. One scientist described what followed as "utter calamity." If an earthquake did hit Sodom and Gomorrah as the model showed, the ground would have turned to quicksand, sending the towns at the edge of the water into a slide that wouldn't end until they reached the bottom of the Dead Sea.

THE DEAD SEA contains **ten times more SALT** than Earth's oceans. The salt concentration is so high that **larger organisms can't survive.** In the Bible, **KING SOLOMON** presented the Queen of Sheba with salts from the Dead Sea.

GENESIS 24

A BRIDE FOR ISAAC

Abraham appreciated his many blessings, but he wished for one more thing before he died—to see his son Isaac married to a woman from his homeland. Abraham summoned his head servant, Eliezer, and sent him on a journey to Haran in Nahor to find Isaac a suitable bride.

Eliezer loaded ten camels with gifts for the bride-to-be and her family. It was customary to pay a bride-price, and Abraham spared no expense.

When Eliezer arrived outside the city, he led his camels to the communal well. It was evening, the time when the women of Nahor made their way to the well to fill their water jugs. Eliezer prayed, "O Lord, God of my master Abraham, please grant me success."

Eliezer was still praying when he saw a beautiful young woman named Rebekah carrying a water jug on her shoulder. Eliezer asked her if he might have a sip of her water. She said, "Drink, my lord." Then she added, "I will water your camels."

She must be the one, Eliezer thought. He offered the young woman a gold nose ring and two gold bracelets, asking, "May I stay in your father's house for the night?"

At Rebekah's home, Eliezer explained his mission to her family. "Will you come with me to marry Isaac?" he asked Rebekah. When Rebekah and her family agreed, Eliezer presented them with gold, silver, and fine clothing.

The next morning, Rebekah and her maids mounted the camels to follow Eliezer home. Isaac saw their caravan approaching and came to greet them.

As a customary sign of their betrothal, Isaac took Rebekah into his mother's tent. Isaac's mother had died, so Rebekah now became the family matriarch. Isaac came to love her.

detail from "Rebekah and Eliezer," by Bartolomé Esteban Murillo, about 1665 C.E.

DID YOU KNOW?

In early biblical days, it was tradition for GROOMS to pay the bride's family for their daughter. Wealthy men might give gold and silver, livestock, or property. Men with little money might work for the bride's family as payment. During the Second Temple period, between 530 B.C.E. and 70 C.E., these payments REVERSED. A DOWRY SYSTEM was created in which the bride's family paid the groom-to-be. Later, both practices ended and the *ketubah* became popular. The ketubah protected the personal money of the husband or wife.

SIBLING RIVALRY

When Rebekah gave birth to twins, the secondborn was holding onto the firstborn's heel. Isaac and Rebekah took one look at their firstborn, covered in red hair, and named him Esau, which means "hairy" in Hebrew. They named their secondborn Jacob, meaning "holder of the heel."

Esau and Jacob had little in common. Esau loved the outdoors and hunted with his father. Jacob liked tending sheep and spending time with his mother. As the older brother, Esau had special privileges, including the birthright to inherit his father's wealth.

One day, Jacob was cooking stew when his brother barged in and demanded, "Give me some stew."

Envious of Esau's privileges, Jacob decided to get even. "I will trade you my stew for your birthright." Esau agreed, and then he ate his fill.

Next, Jacob wanted his father's deathbed blessing, also a privilege for the eldest son and considered good fortune. When Isaac was blind and near death, he called for Esau and told him he would soon give him his blessing. Rebekah heard this and quickly fetched Jacob, as he was her favorite son.

"We'll disguise you so your father thinks you are Esau," Rebekah told Jacob. She dressed him in Esau's coat, smoky from campfires, so Jacob would smell like Esau, and covered his bare skin with hairy goatskins so Jacob would feel like Esau.

Jacob went to receive Isaac's blessing. Isaac touched the hair on Jacob's hands, and then smelled the coat he wore. Believing that this was his eldest son, Isaac blessed Jacob.

When Esau discovered Jacob's trick, he vowed to kill him. But Rebekah sent Jacob to live with her brother far away, leaving Esau with his anger.

"Isaac Blessing Jacob," by Govert Flinck, 1638 C.E.

DID YOU KNOW?

Even in biblical times, people were given **NICKNAMES.** In the Bible, because of his fiery red hair, **Esau's nickname was EDOM, which means "red" in Hebrew.** The nickname must have stuck, because Esau's descendants were called **EDOMITES.** God changed Jacob's name to Israel, and Jacob's descendants were called **ISRAELITES.** Considering the battles that went on between Esau and Jacob, it comes as no surprise that **the Edomites and the Israelites were ENEMIES.** When the **Israelites fled from slavery** in the Book of Exodus, the king of Edom would not let them cross his land. God, however, was not going to let the Israelites hold that against them. **They were, after all, FAMILY.**

DID YOU KNOW?

CHERUBIM are often shown in artwork as **charming, pudgy, little boys with tiny wings.** But in the Bible, these heavenly beings **are described very differently.** When God forced Adam and Eve out of the Garden of Eden, he **sent frightening cherubim to guard the way to the tree of life.** In Ezekiel's vision, cherubim were scary hooved creatures with four-sided heads. And in the sanctuary of Solomon's Temple, they were amazing **15-FOOT (4.5-M)-TALL GIANTS.**

"Jacob's Dream," by Salvator Rosa, 1665 C.E.

GENESIS 28

JACOB'S LADDER

After Jacob tricked his brother, Esau, so he could claim Isaac's blessing, Jacob had to flee Esau's wrath. Jacob left his home of Beersheba, in the southernmost part of the Promised Land, and set out to stay with his uncle in Haran, in what is now southeastern Turkey. Along the way, he had a vision.

It was getting late, and Jacob found himself outside a city called Luz. He decided to lie down for the night. He had just set his head down on the stone he was using for a pillow and closed his eyes when he began to dream. In his dream, Jacob saw a ladder that reached up into heaven. Angels climbed up and down the ladder between heaven and earth.

God stood beside Jacob, telling him that this land would be his and that his many offspring would be blessed and spread all over the Earth—north, south, east, and west. God said, "I will not leave you until I have done what I have promised."

When Jacob woke up, he was frightened by the dream. He realized that he was in a holy place, that this was God's house and the gateway to heaven.

Early the next morning, Jacob set the stone he'd used as a pillow on its end to make a pillar. He rubbed the stone with oil to show it belonged to God and make it holy for worship. He changed the name of the city from Luz to Bethel, which means "house of God."

"If God watches over me, and feeds and clothes me, and allows me to return home safely, then He shall be my God," Jacob vowed. "This place shall be holy."

Before continuing on his journey to new adventures, Jacob pledged a tenth of all his future earnings to God.

SOCIAL LIFE AT THE WELL

In the Bible, places where people could get water were very important. Townspeople often gathered around the town well or a bubbling spring to draw water and share news. Sometimes basins called cisterns served as the water supply. A cistern was often located at the end of an underground tunnel. It might collect rainwater through a hole created in the tunnel ceiling. In some cases, an underground spring might feed into the basin from below.

Women went to the watering holes each day to collect water for their families. Before lifting their full clay pitchers onto their shoulders or heads, they would share a bit of gossip. In the Book of Genesis, Rebekah met the servant of her future husband, Isaac, at a well.

detail from "Rebekah at the Well," by Ottavio Vannini, 1626 C.E.

In the 1960s, archaeologists discovered a massive cistern at Khirbet et Tell, some 12 miles (19.5 km) north of Jerusalem. It dates back to 2500 B.C.E. and held almost as much water as an Olympic-size swimming pool.

More recently, using backhoes, rope pulleys, and other tools, archaeologists removed nearly 500 tons (454 t) of debris to reveal an underground cistern and tunnel that served as a water supply for Gezer, a city in the Judean foothills of Israel during biblical times. People reached this cistern by entering through a keyhole-shaped entrance inside their town and then following a long, sloping tunnel. At 12 feet (3.5 m) wide and 24 feet (7.5 m) tall, the tunnel at Gezer was large enough for two donkeys loaded with water jugs to pass one another coming and going to the cistern below. Similar tunnel-and-cistern systems have been found at other key sites in the Holy Land, including Megiddo, Hazor, and Jerusalem.

Often the tunnel entrance to a cistern was located inside the town walls. This provided the townspeople with access to water during times of war even if the enemy was camped outside the town walls. Ancient builders sometimes lined the cisterns with rock and plastered them with a clay or lime mixture as a liner to keep the water from seeping into the ground. Every drop of water is precious in a desert climate. More than one battle was fought over the control of a water source.

Not all cisterns were underground. To prevent people or animals from falling into a cistern's opening when it was at ground level, townspeople might surround it with a low stone wall or cover it with a stone. Sometimes a cistern went dry. Because cisterns were deep, they were escape-proof, and they could be used as dungeons. In the Book of Jeremiah, soldiers tossed the Prophet Jeremiah into an empty cistern, where he sank into the mud. Rescuers pulled him by rope to safety, but other prisoners may have been less fortunate, left to starve in these deep, dark chambers.

WELLS and water sources served as landmarks for traders and travelers. In the Bible, **MOSES** and the Israelites' route from Egypt to Canaan was often described by their stops at watering holes.

a cistern at Herod's Masada fortress in the Negev, a desert in Israel

DID YOU KNOW?

Some English versions of the Bible mistakenly translated the Hebrew word *me'il,* which means top garment, as "COAT." The New Revised Standard Version of the Bible describes Jacob's gift to Joseph as a "long robe with sleeves." Some experts believe that it was a KNEE-LENGTH garment, woven with colorful threads. Others believe it may have reached to the ANKLES. Shepherds, like Joseph's family, didn't wear long garments that would keep them from moving freely. If it was a long robe that Joseph wore, then that could have been a sign Jacob was grooming his second youngest son to oversee his older brothers, something that wasn't customary and would upset the older brothers.

"Joseph's Coat of Many Colors Brought to His Father, Jacob," English school, 19th century C.E.

GENESIS 37, 39–41

JOSEPH'S ROBE

Jacob had 12 sons, who formed the 12 tribes of Israel, but Joseph was his favorite. Jacob gave Joseph a beautifully made long robe with sleeves. When Joseph's brothers saw this robe, they were jealous and began to plot their revenge.

One day when the brothers were tending their father's flock, they threw Joseph into a pit. Soon afterward, they sold Joseph to a caravan of traders traveling to Egypt, to sell as a slave.

To cover up their evil deed, the brothers slaughtered a goat and soaked Joseph's magnificent robe in its blood to trick their father into thinking Joseph was dead. They took the robe to their father, who was heartbroken when he saw it. "Some ferocious animal has devoured him," Jacob cried.

In Egypt, Joseph was sold to an officer of the pharaoh and worked for him as a slave. One day, he was unjustly accused of a crime and thrown into prison.

Joseph suffered in jail until the pharaoh had a dream that none of his wise men could explain. The royal cupbearer, once a prisoner along with Joseph, remembered that Joseph had correctly translated his dream. He told the pharaoh, and Joseph was summoned.

"I dreamt seven fat cows climbed out of the Nile, followed by seven skinny ones. The skinny cows ate the fat cows. In my next dream the same thing happened, this time with seven ears of grain," said the pharaoh.

Joseph told the pharaoh what God was trying to tell him. "For the next seven years Egypt will enjoy plentiful harvests. Then there will be seven years of famine." Joseph advised the pharaoh to begin storing grain to prepare for the lean years.

The grateful pharaoh placed Joseph in charge of these preparations, gave him fine clothes and jewelry, and made him his governor.

golden bull's head that was part of a lyre, a musical instrument, from the Royal Tombs of Ur

THE GREAT DEATH PIT

Throughout history, different groups of people have created underground tombs and filled them with exquisite clothing and jewels, and these items have endured for millennia. Some of the most beautiful were found at the ancient city of Ur, in today's Iraq, which the Book of Genesis says is Abraham's birthplace.

Archaeologist Leonard Woolley arrived at Ur in late 1922. After studying the landscape, Woolley focused on a hill with the ruins of an ancient temple complex called the Ziggurat of Ur. He dug through centuries' worth of windblown sand and soil, creating two long, narrow trenches. In Trench A, workers uncovered evidence of ancient burials filled with priceless grave goods, jewelry, and skeletons. In Trench B, they found the brick remains of a large building.

This illustration shows a possible reconstruction of buildings at the temple complex at Ur.

Over a span of 12 years, Woolley's team found a temple, the home of a high priestess, and ordinary houses. All these discoveries taught Woolley about life in Ur. Woolley's men also excavated some 1,850 burials, dating to between 2600 B.C.E. and 2000 B.C.E. Woolley determined that 16 of these were royal tombs, based on their grand construction and the lavish goods inside. He found evidence that servants, who were meant to attend to the members of the royal families in death, were buried alongside them in the tomb.

Woolley nicknamed the most spectacular tomb the "great death pit." He found 74 bodies here, including six soldiers with weapons, likely placed at the tomb's entrance to protect it from grave robbers. The other 68 were women, dressed in red and wearing golden headdresses and jewelry. Cosmetics in shells lay beside them. Half of them had drinking cups, as if they were attending a ghoulish banquet. To entertain the "guests," the bodies of six women lay near a harp and two lyres. Because of the way the servants' bodies were dressed and arranged, Woolley guessed that they had voluntarily taken poison. But a recent study of two skulls revealed that a sharp instrument had been driven into them.

Not all tombs in biblical times were as elaborate as Woolley's royal tombs. Family tombs—caves where rock benches were carved out of the walls—were more common in Old Testament times. The dead were placed on the benches, sometimes wearing expensive clothing. After the body had decomposed, the bones were stored at the back of the tomb to make room for a new burial. Because the Law of Moses regarded a dead body as "unclean," tombs and other graves were located outside the town walls.

Not everyone could afford even a modest family tomb. A mass grave was the poor person's final resting place. Criminals and enemies might just have a few stones stacked above them to mark their grave.

Instead of treasures, archaeologists usually uncover **items of daily life.** In tombs at **TELL EN-NASBEH,** northwest of Jerusalem, archaeologists found **tools for weaving cloth** from 1200 to 100 B.C.E.

"Barak and Deborah," by Francesco Solimena, about 1730 C.E.

DID YOU KNOW?

Today when we think of **judges,** we think of black robes and courtrooms where the judge presides over a trial. But the **DUTIES OF JUDGES IN THE BIBLE** were much broader. Judges often were **military leaders** battling against oppressors.

JUDGES 4–5

WOMEN IN WAR

For 20 years, Jabin, the Canaanite king of Hazor, had oppressed the Israelites. They wanted to rise up against him, but Jabin's army was strong. It had 900 iron chariots and was led by the skilled commander Sisera.

The Israelites looked to Deborah for help. She was a famed prophetess (one who foretold the future) and also the only female judge in the land. Israelite judges were leaders of the people, but because Deborah was a woman, she could not lead the army. She used a man named Barak to carry out her orders. She told Barak that God had given this command: "Take 10,000 fighting men to Mount Tabor and hold your position until I draw Sisera and his army out to meet you along the Kishon River. There you will engage in battle and defeat them."

"I'll go," Barak said, "if you come with me."

"I will go," replied Deborah, "but be aware that a woman, not a man, will earn the glory for this victory."

When Sisera heard that Deborah was gathering an army, he advanced on Mount Tabor to crush her militia. Just as Sisera's chariots approached the Kishon River, the skies opened, sending down a violent rainstorm. The waters of a flash flood drowned his charioteers.

Barak charged, leading 10,000 soldiers against Sisera's army until they were slain. Only Sisera escaped. He fled to a nearby herder's camp.

Jael, the wife of a herder, greeted Sisera. "Have no fear," she said. She welcomed him into her tent and said she would guard the door while he slept.

Once Sisera drifted off to sleep, Jael crept up to him and killed him with a sharp tent peg. Deborah's prophecy—that a woman would earn the glory for the victory—was fulfilled.

DEEPWATER DISCOVERY

In 1999, a submarine off the coast of Israel searched the seafloor for a sunken Israeli submarine. Investigators on board noticed fuzzy images of what looked like two ancient shipwrecks. They notified marine archaeologist Robert Ballard, who is famous for discovering many shipwrecks, including the *Titanic*. Ballard in turn notified biblical archaeologist Lawrence Stager. The two put together a team of oceanographers and archaeologists. They loaded sonar equipment and a remote-controlled, deepwater submersible named *Jason* onto a research ship and set out for the underwater site.

Because of a lack of technology until now, marine archaeologists (scientists who study remains left underwater by humans) who wanted to learn about ships' trade routes in biblical times had worked only on shallow-water shipwrecks. But tides and currents often forced those wrecks onto their sides, broke them up, and scattered or destroyed their contents. Anything that remained was often looted by treasure hunters.

Ships that sank in deeper waters offered more. They remained upright on the seafloor and lay undisturbed in the calmer depths. Although the ships' wood rotted or was eaten away by shipworms, their cargo remained as it was stored centuries before.

Ballard, Stager, and the team crowded into the control room of the research vessel. All eyes were on the video screens as *Jason*'s underwater cameras relayed high-resolution photographs of the seafloor. Image after image of clay jars called amphoras filled the screen. By the grin on Stager's face, Ballard knew the amphoras were old—very old.

Based on the amphoras, Stager worked to determine each ship's age, origin, cargo, and likely destination. He determined that these amphoras were Phoenician when he found in them a certain kind of alga that grows only on the coast near the ancient Phoenician port cities of Tyre, Sidon, and Byblos, in today's Lebanon. Stager knew that Phoenicians had been trading along the seacoast and delivering goods to Solomon, King of Israel, as early as 970 B.C.E. Then around 750–700 B.C.E., two Phoenician trading ships, possibly part of a fleet, may have sailed from Tyre, in Phoenicia, to Ashkelon, in Israel, then headed to Egypt to deliver their goods. These ships probably ran into a violent storm and sank. Each ship carried 400 amphoras, stacked in rows with a rope running through their handles to keep them secure. Could these be the Phoenician trading ships?

Phoenician pottery jars often held oil or wine for trade on ships sailing from Tyre to Egypt.

This discovery off the coast of Israel confirmed biblical stories of trade connections between Tyre and Israel. In the second Book of Samuel, King Hiram of Tyre sent cedarwood, cypress, and builders to construct Solomon's Temple in Israel. And in the Book of Ezekiel, the Prophet Ezekiel described the ruin of a ship, similar to these, that came from ancient Tyre.

TRADE ROUTES stretched across the biblical world. **Camel caravans** brought goods **BY LAND** and **ships carried goods by sea.**

A replica of a Phoenician ship sails along the coast of the Mediterranean.

DID YOU KNOW?

Archaeobotanists are scientists who study plant remains found at archaeological excavations to learn how ancient people used plants in their daily lives. ABRAHAM'S BALM is one name for a plant that grows throughout all of Israel except in the Negev desert. Because of its water-seeking roots, this plant is able to thrive even when not near a body of water. Some archaeobotanists believe Abraham's balm may be the plant referred to in Leviticus 23:40 as the "willows of the brook."

detail from "The Finding of Moses," by Nicolas Poussin, 1651 C.E.

EXODUS 2

AMONG THE BULRUSHES

When Jacob's descendants arrived in Egypt, they were only 70 strong. With each generation their numbers grew, until they spread across the eastern Nile Delta. The Israelites multiplied so rapidly that the pharaoh became alarmed. He worried that they might join forces with Egypt's enemies to fight against him.

To protect himself, the pharaoh enslaved them and made them do hard labor. Still their population grew.

Next, the pharaoh ordered Israelite midwives to kill every male born under their care. But the midwives, fearing God more than the pharaoh, spared God's favored children. Desperate now, the pharaoh ordered all of his subjects to throw every newborn Israelite boy into the Nile.

In these harsh times, Jochebed and her husband, Amram, had their third child and second son. In order to try to save him from the pharaoh, Jochebed lined a papyrus basket with bitumen and pitch to waterproof it. She placed her three-month-old in the basket and set him adrift among the reeds along the Nile. From a distance, her daughter Miriam watched.

Soon the pharaoh's daughter came to the river's edge to bathe. She spied the floating basket and sent one of her attendants to fetch it. The sweet crying baby tugged at the princess's heart. "This must be an Israelite child," she said.

With that, Miriam boldly stepped out from hiding. "Shall I find an Israelite woman to nurse him?" she asked. When the pharaoh's daughter agreed, Miriam ran to find her mother.

The princess told Miriam's mother to take the child and be its nurse. The princess would pay for his care. Jochebed cuddled the baby who was her own, now named Moses by the princess. Safely, under royal protection, Moses grew up as the princess's son.

detail from a fresco depicting a funeral feast with musicians, in the tomb of Rekhmire, Luxor, Egypt

STORIES FROM THE GRAVE

Experts studying mummies from ancient Egypt can piece together the health of those who lived in biblical times. Health, and sometimes a long life, depended on your station in life. A wealthy person and the common worker led far different lifestyles.

Everyday life for most people was not easy, and their skeletons show it. Common laborers often ended up with damaged spines from carrying heavy loads. Poor diets made them malnourished. Experts found evidence of this in the bones of a weaver named Nakht (his name and occupation were inscribed on his coffin). His shinbones were marked with stress lines, showing that he did not get enough food for long periods. He also had parasites—organisms that may enter a person through the legs or feet and then feed off the body's organs.

Nakht died at about age 65, likely from pneumonia that attacked his already diseased lungs. Although Nakht had been lovingly buried—someone shaved his face, trimmed his nails, and wrapped his body—he was not embalmed, or mummified. His family probably couldn't afford the expensive process to create a mummy, which involved preserving the body and its organs with oils, minerals, and spices.

Wealthy people still had health problems, even though their lifestyles were luxurious. Experts studied the mummy of the pharaoh Ramses II, who may have been pharaoh at the time Moses led the Israelites out of Egypt. They found wounds and old fractures from battles and hunting. The arthritis in his neck and spine would have made him walk hunched over for the last ten years of his life. A hole in his jaw shows that he had a serious tooth infection that could have killed him. Still, the pharaoh lived to the ripe old age of 90—a very long life for an Egyptian or anyone at the time. Most people didn't live past 40.

Inside this coffin, the 2,700-year-old mummy of the temple singer Asru rests in the Manchester Museum in England.

In addition to the very rich and very poor, there were people in the middle who had jobs that did not require physical labor. A woman whom experts call Asru was in this group. After studying her mummy and coffin inscriptions, experts determined that Asru was a temple singer. Professional singing in the Old Testament goes back to King David (1040 B.C.E.–940 B.C.E.). Asru's hands show little wear, indicating she was pampered. Still, she suffered from medical problems.

X-rays show that Asru's spine was damaged and that the bone behind her ear was abnormal. She would have suffered back pain and earaches. Scientists found a cyst in her lung caused by a tapeworm. She would have coughed and wheezed, with the constant chest pain maybe forcing her to stop singing. A parasite had laid eggs in her stomach, which would have given Asru severe stomachaches. She may have had bone cancer and diabetes. Despite all this, Asru's arteries, teeth, and bones show that she lived to be 50 or 60 years old.

The **Israelites never practiced embalming,** or artificially preserving, bodies. **JACOB AND JOSEPH** were the only two that the Bible says were embalmed—much like the pharaohs were—**because of their ties to Egypt.**

DID YOU KNOW?

THE NILE TURNING BLOOD-RED is described in an ancient Egyptian papyrus called the Admonitions of Ipuwer. Scientists think this could have been caused by RED CLAY that washed into the Nile after heavy rains, or by the growth of a red algae bloom. Either event could have led to a series of plagues. FISH would suffocate and die from the clay or algae. FROGS would escape, looking for clean water. FLIES would swarm over the rotting fish and pick up a poison the fish gave off called ANTHRAX. This would kill livestock and cause boil-like wounds on people's skin.

"Seventh Plague of Egypt," by John Martin, 1823 C.E.

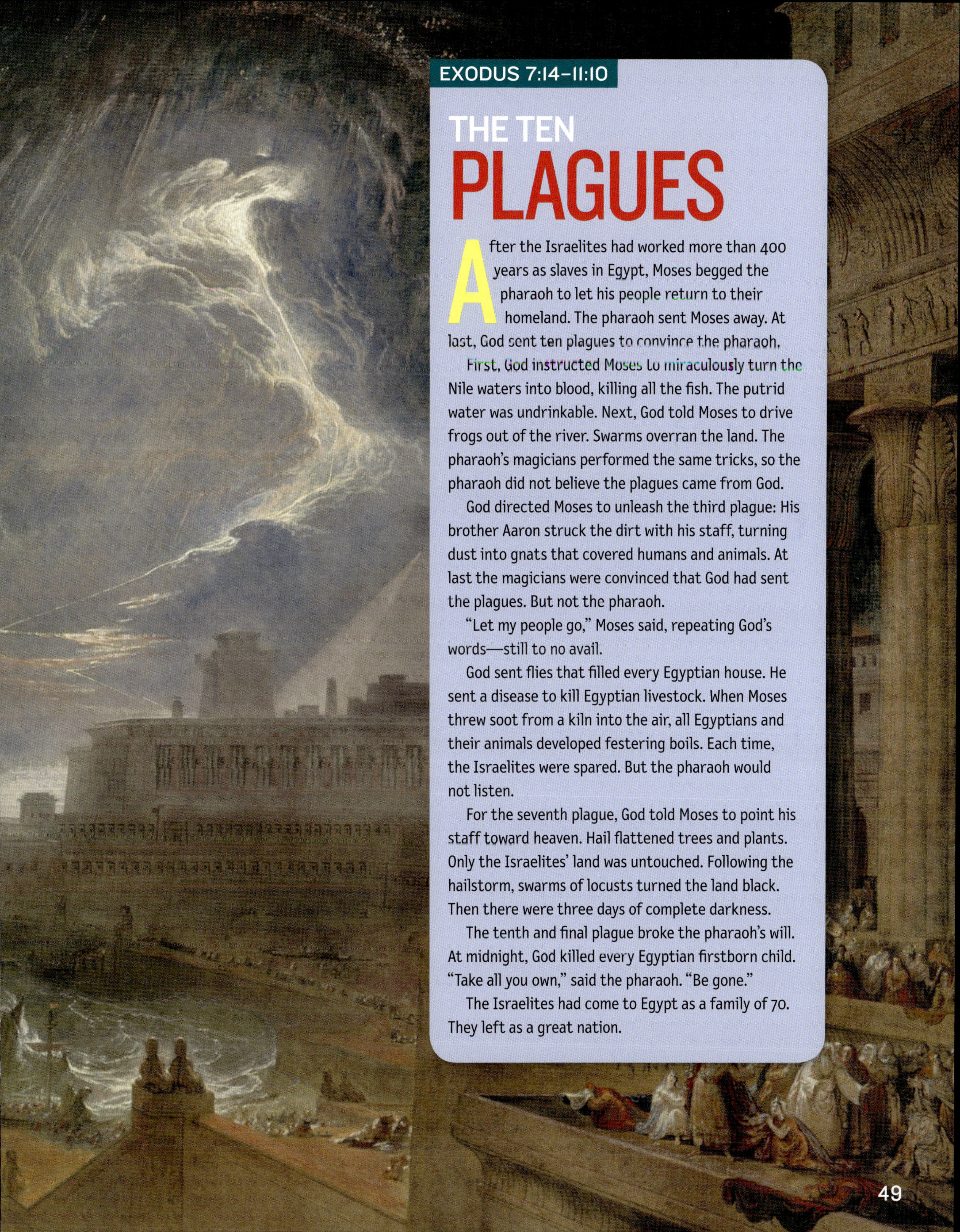

EXODUS 7:14–11:10

THE TEN PLAGUES

After the Israelites had worked more than 400 years as slaves in Egypt, Moses begged the pharaoh to let his people return to their homeland. The pharaoh sent Moses away. At last, God sent ten plagues to convince the pharaoh.

First, God instructed Moses to miraculously turn the Nile waters into blood, killing all the fish. The putrid water was undrinkable. Next, God told Moses to drive frogs out of the river. Swarms overran the land. The pharaoh's magicians performed the same tricks, so the pharaoh did not believe the plagues came from God.

God directed Moses to unleash the third plague: His brother Aaron struck the dirt with his staff, turning dust into gnats that covered humans and animals. At last the magicians were convinced that God had sent the plagues. But not the pharaoh.

"Let my people go," Moses said, repeating God's words—still to no avail.

God sent flies that filled every Egyptian house. He sent a disease to kill Egyptian livestock. When Moses threw soot from a kiln into the air, all Egyptians and their animals developed festering boils. Each time, the Israelites were spared. But the pharaoh would not listen.

For the seventh plague, God told Moses to point his staff toward heaven. Hail flattened trees and plants. Only the Israelites' land was untouched. Following the hailstorm, swarms of locusts turned the land black. Then there were three days of complete darkness.

The tenth and final plague broke the pharaoh's will. At midnight, God killed every Egyptian firstborn child. "Take all you own," said the pharaoh. "Be gone."

The Israelites had come to Egypt as a family of 70. They left as a great nation.

HOW COULD THE RED SEA PART?

One of the most dramatic stories in the Bible is the Exodus—the story of Moses leading the Israelites out of Egypt with the pharaoh and his army in hot pursuit. And one of the most exciting moments in that story is the parting of the Red Sea.

Trapped between the Egyptian army and the Red Sea with 600 chariots chasing him and the Israelites, Moses raised one hand out over the sea. God sent a strong east wind to clear a path between two towering walls of water so the Israelites could run to safety. Once they reached the opposite shore, Moses raised his hand once again, and the waters rushed back, swallowing up the Egyptian chariots and sending the Egyptians to a watery grave.

detail from "The Crossing of the Red Sea," by Luca Giordano, about 1682 C.E.

Oceanographers and geologists have discussed what could cause dry land to suddenly appear in the middle of the Red Sea. Some think a pathway was created by volcanic eruptions and huge waves called tsunamis that might follow. Although a tsunami could create the conditions described in the Bible—one moment no water, the next a swell that covers up an entire army—there is no evidence to show that there was a volcanic eruption or a tsunami at this time in history. But what about the wind? The Bible states that an east wind parted the sea.

A Russian oceanographer set out to determine if wind alone could create the conditions that would have cleared a pathway for Moses. Choosing a location in the northern part of the Red Sea's Gulf of Suez, he calculated that it would take four hours for 600,000 Israelites to cross from one coast to the other. His math showed that if the wind reached at least 67 miles an hour (108 km/h), it would uncover a reef below the surface of the water. The reef could have provided a dry path for the Israelites, but chariots would have had a hard time crossing it.

Other researchers point to a phenomenon called a "wind setdown" to explain the Bible story. Strong, ongoing winds can cause a huge drop in sea level. In the 1800s, a wind setdown in the Nile Delta pushed aside water five feet (1.5 m) deep to expose dry land.

After studying archaeological records and satellite maps, researchers developed computer models to show how the wind could have parted the water for the Israelites. The models showed wind speeds of 63 miles an hour (101 km/h) all through the night. These winds pushed back water that was six feet (2 m) deep and exposed mudflats that were two miles (3 km) long and three miles (5 km) wide. It lasted long enough that the Israelites would have been able to cross to safety. Once the winds stopped, the water rushed back, showing that anyone left behind—like the Egyptian army—would have been in danger.

Early written accounts say the **Israelites were trapped** between the army and the *yam suph*, or **"SEA OF REEDS,"** not the Red Sea. **People, but not heavy chariots,** could have crossed the soft floor exposed by wind.

Reeds dot the sandbanks of the Bitter Lakes, which scholars believe is the "sea of reeds" where the waters parted for the Israelites, previously translated as "Red Sea."

DID YOU KNOW?

In this story from the Bible, **THERE WAS NO WATER AT REPHIDIM,** where the Israelites camped after the first manna—food provided by God. **The thirsty people were ready to stone Moses to death.**

God told Moses **to strike a certain rock** with the same staff Aaron had used to cause the plagues in Egypt. **WATER GUSHED FROM THE ROCK** for all the Israelites to quench their thirst. Moses called the place **MASSAH, which means "testing,"** and **MERIBAH, which means "quarreling,"** because the Israelites had been tested and they quarreled throughout the journey out of Egypt.

In the southern Sinai desert, **an oasis at the Wadi Feiran** is thought to be the place called Rephidim. **Legend says a nearby rock is the one Moses struck for water.**

"Moses and the Israelites Gathering of Manna," by unknown artist, 16th century C.E., in the Cathedral of Santa Maria Assunta, Padua, Italy

EXODUS 16:1–27

WHAT IS IT?

A month after they'd escaped the Egyptians, the Israelites were still trudging through the desert. There was no water or food anywhere. Forgetting the harshness of slavery, they complained to Moses and Aaron: "At least in Egypt we had our fill of bread, better than starving out here in the desert."

God told Moses that he would provide for the Israelites. At sunset he would send meat, and every morning bread would fall from heaven. The Israelites could collect all they needed for the day—but only for the one day. On the sixth day, however, they could gather twice as much. This was a test, God told Moses, to see if they followed his instructions faithfully.

That evening, the Israelites' camp was covered in quail. The next morning when the dew lifted, the ground was covered with a powder of flakes so fine that it looked as if it had snowed. The white flakes tasted like wafers made with honey. They called the flakes manna, which is Hebrew for "what is it?"

Moses instructed the Israelites: "Eat all that you gather; don't save any for tomorrow."

Not everyone listened to Moses. Those who saved extra found it spoiled and filled with worms the next day.

On the sixth day, Moses said, "Tomorrow we will rest because it is the Holy Sabbath Day in honor of the Lord. Cook enough today for tomorrow. There will be no quail or bread on the Sabbath." The next day, those who did not listen went searching for food. They found nothing.

For 40 years the Israelites wandered in the desert, and God gave them manna. He told Moses to keep a serving of manna for future generations, so it was stored in a gold jar and placed in the Ark of the Covenant with the Ten Commandments.

EXODUS 19:1–24, 20

MOSES AND THE TEN COMMANDMENTS

For three months, God had taken care of the Israelites on their journey from Egypt through the desert to Mount Sinai. There, God would reveal himself to them.

The people camped in front of the mountain. Over the next few days, Moses climbed the mountain many times to speak with God. The first time, God told Moses that if the people obeyed his words and kept his covenant, they would be his "treasured possession out of all the peoples." Everyone agreed to obey God.

On the next climb, God told Moses that in three days he would appear in a dark cloud and that the people would be able to hear his voice. Only Moses and Aaron were to climb the mountain or touch it. Any other person would be killed.

For three days, the Israelites prepared to be in God's presence. They washed their clothes and purified themselves. On the third day, the Israelites awoke to trumpet blasts so loud they trembled with fear. Thunder shook the Earth and lightning lit the sky. A cloud of smoke enveloped Mount Sinai.

Moses climbed to speak a third time to God. God answered in thunder. When Moses returned to fetch Aaron, he found the Israelites quaking in fear. "Don't be afraid," Moses said. "God just wants to keep you from sinning."

Moses, Aaron, and other elders walked to the foot of the mountain, and then Moses went alone into the cloud to speak again with God. God instructed Moses on the laws he wanted the people to follow. He gave Moses the Ten Commandments on two stone tablets to take to the people.

God also gave Moses other laws about how to live a good life and told Moses how to worship him. The people promised to obey, and they built a carrying case for the tablets called the Ark of the Covenant.

"Moses Presenting the Ten Commandments," a fresco by the School of Raphael, early 1500s C.E., in St. Peter's Basilica, Vatican City

DID YOU KNOW?

The oldest known record of laws is from the **SUMERIAN CITY OF UR** in the 21st century B.C.E. That's long before Moses could have received the Ten Commandments and other laws on Mount Sinai.

THE LAND OF MILK AND HONEY

After God's dramatic appearance at Mount Sinai in the Book of Exodus, God commanded Moses to lead the Israelites to "the land flowing with milk and honey." This beautiful area, called Canaan, lay between the Mediterranean Sea and the River Jordan. Here the Book of Genesis tells us lived the descendants of Noah.

Canaan's fertile valleys and pasturelands with many water sources provided the perfect conditions for growing food, tending livestock that produced milk, and raising bees for honey. No wonder it was called the land of milk and honey. The towns also welcomed trade caravans. Canaanites grew wealthy trading their foods, goods, and services.

Ancient beehives found by archaeologists in Israel uphold the idea of a "land of milk and honey."

One Canaanite town has become a major excavation site in Israel, Tel Rehov. Archaeologists have unearthed hundreds of ceramic vessels, altars, figurines, weapons, and beads dating from the tenth to the ninth century B.C.E., the time of Kings David and Solomon. They've found walls, courtyards, houses, ovens, and benches. But nothing was as surprising as the discovery of a beehouse for hundreds of beehives.

All the beehives were clay cylinders of the same size, made from straw and animal dung. Each hive was large enough to hold almost 15 gallons (57 L) of honey. The top of the hive had a hole in the center for bees to fly in and out. The bottom of the hive had an opening covered by a lid that the beekeeper could easily remove by its handle to scoop out honeycombs while standing safely opposite the fly hole. The long rows of beehives were stacked three high. Some experts estimate there may once have been more than 200 hives that housed over a million bees. If this is true, then the people were collecting more than half a ton (450 kg) of honey a year for themselves and to trade.

Honey was certainly in demand in ancient times. The Egyptians used honey as a medicine to spread on cuts, as a sweetener, and in rituals. Along with many other cultures, the Babylonians and the Egyptians placed jars of honey in tombs as part of their burial practice to feed the dead in the afterlife.

Just 15 feet (4.5 m) from the beehives, archaeologists at Tel Rehov discovered an altar and objects used for worship. The Canaanites, like the Egyptians, worshipped many gods. The most revered gods were those associated with plentiful harvests. The chalices and bowls found alongside the altar suggest some sort of honey-making ritual to make sure the bees would continue producing honey.

Caravans on their way to market in the ancient cities of Babylon in Mesopotamia, and Thebes in Egypt, must have stopped along the way to buy honey in Canaan. Such an organized operation, with its many beehives producing enough honey to trade, shows that beekeeping was a key industry in this ancient town.

When traveling overland, **TRADERS** often transported their wares by **donkey caravans.** It was not uncommon to have **300 OR MORE DONKEYS** in a caravan.

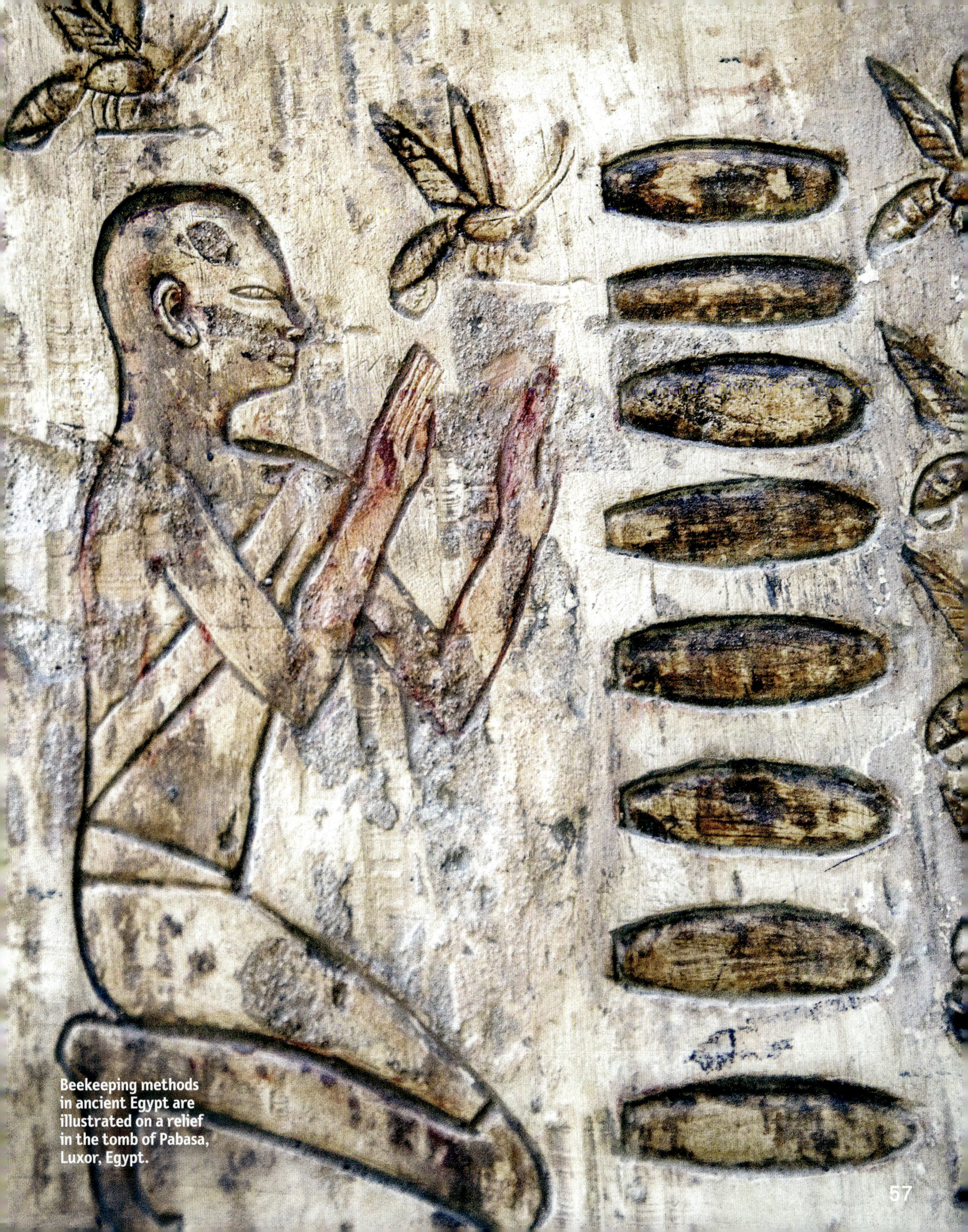

Beekeeping methods in ancient Egypt are illustrated on a relief in the tomb of Pabasa, Luxor, Egypt.

archaeological excavations at the site of ancient Jericho, called Tell es-Sultan

AND THE WALLS CAME TUMBLING DOWN

The Book of Joshua tells about Joshua, who led the Israelites after Moses died. One of God's first commands for Joshua was to invade the city of Jericho and claim it for the faithful. But when Joshua and the Israelites approached the city, they found a massive wall encircling it.

The Book of Joshua goes on to say that Joshua followed God's specific instructions and led the Israelite army in a march around the city once a day for six days. On the seventh day, just as God had instructed, they circled the city wall seven times. On the seventh loop around, Joshua ordered, "Shout!" The entire army shouted at the top of their lungs, and the priests trumpeted their ram's horns at full volume. The walls came tumbling down.

Walls are falling down in this painting by William Brassey Hole of the destruction of Jerusalem.

What do scientists think really happened to towns like Jericho when they were overtaken and the buildings lay in ruin? If the location was a good one, people built a new town on top of the debris from the old one. This building and rebuilding happened many times, as it did to the site of the ancient city of Jericho. Eventually, the rebuilding created a mound higher than the surrounding landscape. Archaeologists call this mound a tell (or tel), from the Arabic word *tall* (pronounced taw), meaning a mound made by humans living there.

Today the site of Jericho is called Tell es-Sultan. Archaeologists have been digging through the layers here and have identified more than 20 different towns. Clearly, this was a favorite location: Mountains rise up on either side, giving natural protection from invaders, and water flows from the nearby River Jordan. Jericho attracted people who had families, farmed, raised animals, and—most important for archaeologists—made pots.

All over this ancient site, archaeologists have found potsherds—broken pieces of pottery—that are filled with information. By studying tiny fragments that were once someone's water jug or soup bowl, archaeologists can determine when many of these sites were settled.

The study of potsherds began in the late 1800s with archaeologist Flinders Petrie, who is nicknamed the "father of pots." Before him, archaeologists considered potsherds nothing more than trash. But Petrie realized their value. He discovered that it was possible to match pot-making designs and methods to specific time periods and cultures. So today, when archaeologists find potsherds at an excavation site, they have meaningful clues as to when the people lived and made them.

Recently, archaeologists have begun the restoration of Jericho's fortifications. Some of these walls suffered damage from massive earthquakes or devastating fires or enemy attacks. After each catastrophe, the city of Jericho was rebuilt, creating another layer in Tell es-Sultan.

Experts continue debating how discoveries of the past century at Tell es-Sultan connect to the story of Jericho, but there is no doubt the walls did come tumbling down.

Dating as far back as **9000 B.C.E.,** Jericho could be the **OLDEST CITY IN THE WORLD.** At 670 feet (204 m) below sea level, it is **the world's lowest city** and is the earliest known city with fortified walls.

DANIEL 6

THROWN TO THE LIONS

After the destruction of Jerusalem by the Babylonians under King Nebuchadnezzar, Darius, the new king of Persia (now Iran), in turn conquered Babylon. He ruled over an empire of 120 provinces. To help manage his kingdom, Darius appointed three administrators. One proved superior to the others. His name was Daniel. He was a young Israelite exile who had been forced from his country and into the Babylon court to serve the foreign king.

Daniel worked hard, and he was honest and faithful. The king planned to put him in charge of his entire kingdom. The other two administrators grew jealous and plotted to destroy Daniel. They watched his every move.

Three times every day, Daniel climbed to the top floor of his house, threw open the windows facing the direction of his home in Jerusalem, and got down on his knees to pray to God. The administrators devised a plan to use his prayers against him.

"King Darius," they said, "you should make a law that punishes whoever prays to anyone but you. Lawbreakers should be thrown to the lions."

Once Darius signed the law, the conspirators caught Daniel praying—as they knew they would—and reported him to the king. The king was upset. He tried to think of some way to rescue Daniel, but the law was the law.

"May your God, whom you faithfully serve, deliver you," the king told Daniel as the guards sealed the lions' den with a boulder. The next morning, Darius rushed to the den, calling to Daniel, "Was your God able to save you?"

Miraculously, Daniel answered. "My God sent an angel to shut the lions' mouths so they could not hurt me." Daniel stepped out, not a scratch on him.

Darius was overjoyed that Daniel had survived, and he was furious at the administrators who had caused this. "Throw Daniel's accusers into the den," Darius ordered. "And their families, too."

"Daniel in the Lions' Den," by Peter Paul Rubens, about 1615 C.E.

DID YOU KNOW?

Many great figures in the Bible faced EXILE—Cain, Jacob, Joseph, Moses, and Jesus, to name a few. Being an exile—**that is, one kept from one's homeland—is a repeated theme in the Bible.** The Book of Daniel tells about the hardships of people exiled from Israel and forced to work in Babylon. Daniel's story sends a message that those who remain strong in their faith—despite injustices—**WILL WIN IN THE END.**

A relief at the temple complex of Karnak, near Luxor, Egypt, shows Ramses II in his war chariot at the Battle of Kadesh.

WAR ON WHEELS

Soon after donkey carts were invented, military leaders decided to use the carts for warfare. They called them chariots. The Bible mentions chariots beginning with the Book of Genesis. Archaeologists have discovered that as early as 2100 B.C.E., they replaced the donkeys with faster horses. Around 1800 B.C.E., the drivers, called charioteers, raced these carts across the plains of Mesopotamia and plowed into enemy armies.

A smaller, ancient version of today's tanks, chariots sent enemies running and created chaos. One charioteer drove, another held a shield for protection, and a third shot arrows at the enemy. Early chariots were hard to maneuver, but they were faster than a man on foot and were deadly against infantry.

In the Royal Tombs of Ur, archaeologist Leonard Woolley discovered a rectangular box decorated with ivory figures and designs, including an early chariot. Because Woolley found the box beside a pole, he thought the box was carried on the end of the pole like an army's flag, called a standard. The box became known as the Standard of Ur, but it's probably just a box. One side of the box shows the battle and the other side shows the surrender and victory banquet. The war panel shows a four-wheeled chariot running over the bodies of the slain enemy while the infantry attacks with spears and axes. Woolley also uncovered chariots buried with warriors and kings and their servants, animals, and drivers.

Pharaoh Ramses II heads a charge on Nubian rebels in this illustration.

In the 1600s B.C.E., the Hyksos, a people from the north, invaded Egypt. They came by chariot, wearing body armor and leather helmets. The chariot gave the Hyksos an advantage, and they won many battles—but not for long. The Egyptians stole the chariot design and improved on it. They made it lighter, which made it easier and faster to drive. They covered the wooden axle with metal so it turned smoothly. They opened up the back of the chariot so that charioteers could easily leap out and fight enemy soldiers in hand-to-hand combat. Solid wood wheels were replaced with lighter wheels that had spokes made of wet cow intestines. When the intestines dried, they shrank and hardened like wood, making a strong connection to the hub, or center, of the wheel.

One famous chariot battle was the Battle of Kadesh, a city in Canaan, fought in 1274 B.C.E. The Hittites (a people from Anatolia, in today's Turkey) had taken control of this Egyptian walled city. To retake it, Pharaoh Ramses II led his army and chariots 1,000 miles (1,600 km). The battle is documented on Ramses II's funeral temple at Abu Simbel as well as at the temple complex of Karnak, near Luxor.

The temple inscriptions show a regal and fearless Ramses in his golden chariot, gripping the reins to his horses. His hair blows in the wind as he races forward. Menna, his faithful shield-bearer, rides beside him. Ramses leads 20,000 infantrymen and charioteers. During battle, Ramses was separated from his forces and (by his own account) single-handedly slaughtered thousands of enemy soldiers.

Who won the Battle of Kadesh? Ramses claimed he did. The Hittite king claimed he did, too! Finally, the two negotiated **THE WORLD'S FIRST PEACE TREATY.** Royal scribes recorded it on **two silver tablets.**

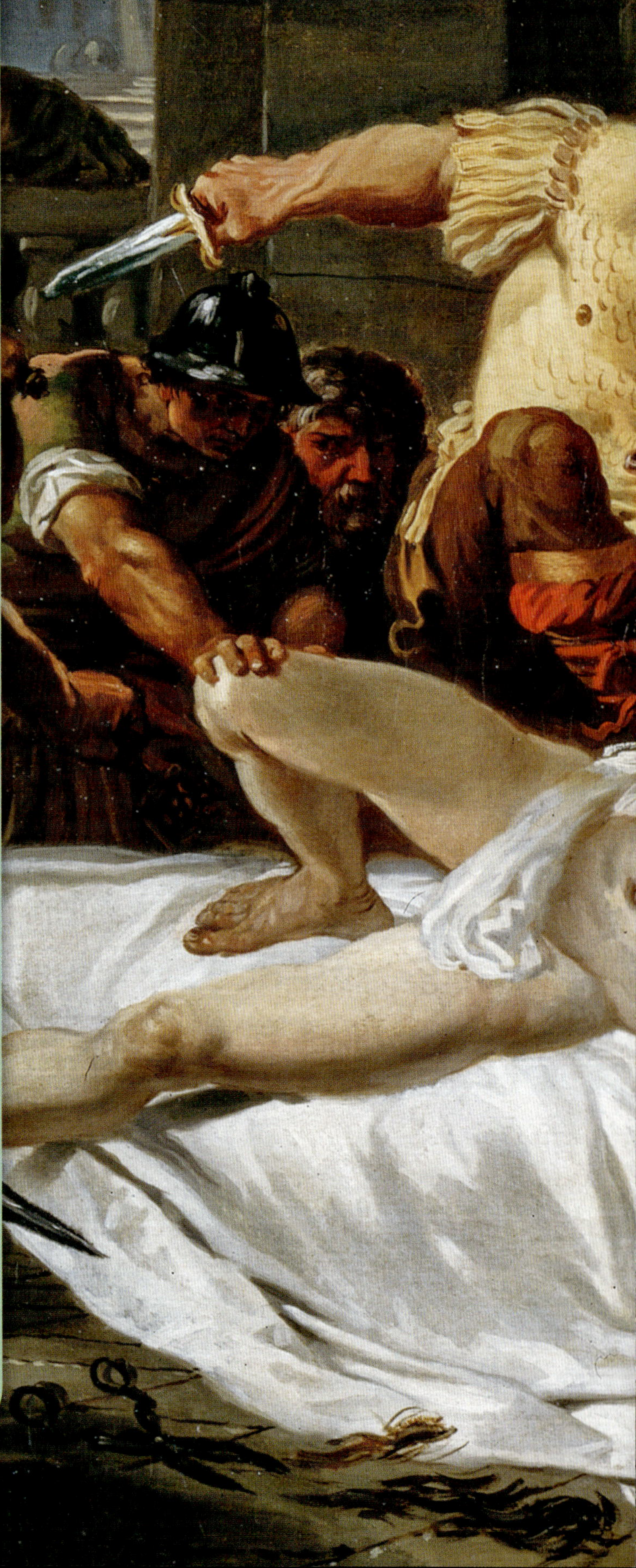

"Samson Betrayed by Delilah," by Felice Giani, 1784 C.E.

JUDGES 16

SAMSON AND DELILAH

Samson was a famous Israelite judge—a leader of the people—known for his great strength. He had torn apart a lion with his bare hands, killed 30 men in anger over a riddle, torched a town for revenge, killed 1,000 men with the jawbone of a donkey, and carried a city gate on his shoulders for 40 miles (64 km) to escape the Philistines, the enemy of the Israelites. Samson led the Israelites for 20 years and worked to keep the Philistines from invading their land. These warriors had a superior army and weapons, but the strong Samson was a thorn in their side.

Samson belonged to a group of Israelites called the Nazarites. They were supposed to follow certain rules—no touching dead animals, no drinking wine, and *no cutting hair.* Samson broke all the rules except for haircutting. His hair was the source of his incredible strength, but the Philistines didn't know it.

When Samson fell in love with a Philistine woman named Delilah, the Philistine leaders offered Delilah money to find out what gave Samson his strength. They knew this was the only way to capture him. Delilah finally got the answer. "If my head were shaved," Samson told her, "I would be weak like everyone else."

While Samson slept, Delilah arranged to have his head shaved. The Philistines then seized the helpless Samson, gouged out his eyes to make him obedient, and chained him. They bound him to a grinding wheel, forcing him to trudge in endless circles grinding flour.

At a festival, they proudly paraded Samson and then chained him to two temple pillars. Samson's hair had begun to grow back, and he prayed for strength—just one more time—to take revenge. With all his might he pulled the pillars down. The temple collapsed, killing Samson and 3,000 Philistines.

DID YOU KNOW?

From artifacts they left, we know the **PHILISTINES** had **an advanced culture and were among the first people to use iron. STRONG IRON TOOLS AND WEAPONS** gave them an advantage over the Israelites, who were still using the softer metal bronze. **IRON TOOLS** made plowing land and cutting wood more efficient. **IRON CHARIOTS AND WEAPONS** resulted in military victories. Once the Israelites discovered the secret of how to smelt, or manufacture, iron, **they finally began to defeat the Philistines.**

"Compiling and Editing the Canon of Scripture From Ancient Documents and Records," by William Brassey Hole (1846–1917), date unknown

ROYAL WRITERS

Scribes in the biblical world performed many duties—historian, diplomat, lawyer, teacher, translator, and draftsman. The profession was handed down from father to son. In Mesopotamia, training to be a scribe took many hours in school bent over a small tablet, using a sharp stick—a stylus—to inscribe or scratch text into clay. In Egypt, apprentices would learn to carefully write with paintbrushes and ink made from charcoal and dirt on paper made from the papyrus plant. Copying texts allowed students to learn the languages of the times. They would erase the clay tablets with a wet rag, or take a new piece of papyrus, and begin again until their teachers were satisfied. School was followed by years of apprenticeship serving under a working scribe. Scribes were society's most educated group of people, not just in writing but also in mathematics, astronomy, and history. They enjoyed a privileged status in the royal court. In the Bible, scribes are often mentioned working alongside the chief priests.

Royal scribes held one of the most important government positions. They were responsible for writing everything that the king asked them to, including important agreements or private letters between his kingdom and other kingdoms. They often needed to read the responses to the king, because few people other than scribes could read—not even royalty. Scribes also had to know more than one language. That's because different kingdoms often had different languages.

For example, the Israelites spoke and wrote in Hebrew, while the Neo-Assyrians and then the Neo-Babylonians in Mesopotamia used the Akkadian language. A scribe from Israel or Judah had to be fluent not only in Hebrew but also in Akkadian, just as a scribe in Mesopotamia might need to know Hebrew, because all sorts of people needed to send letters and other documents back and forth.

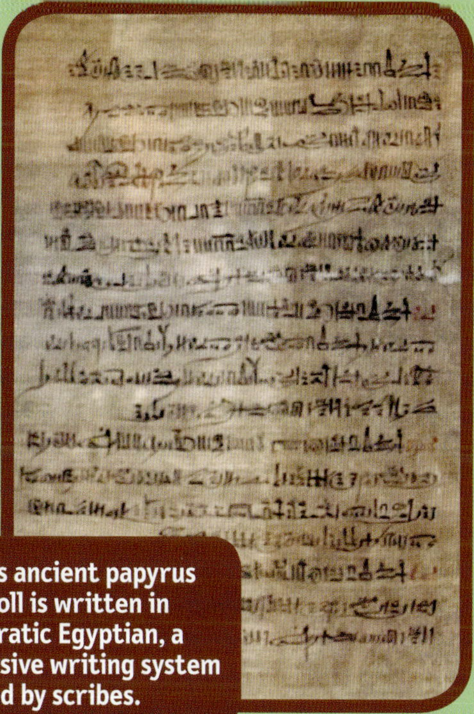

This ancient papyrus scroll is written in hieratic Egyptian, a cursive writing system used by scribes.

Scribes whose leaders were allies with Egypt would have to learn the complicated hieroglyphs used there. Scribes working with Egypt also learned a system of writing for documents known as hieratic. This was writing in cursive hieroglyphs. All scribes in the Middle East would have been trained in Akkadian, too—the language of ancient Sumer. They studied this language much like people study Latin today.

Royal scribes also acted as historians, chronicling the lives of the monarchs in their kingdoms. From the Bible's second Book of Kings we know that the Book of the Annals of the Kings of Israel was a more detailed account of the reigns of Israel's monarchs; II Kings 15:11 states, "Now the rest of the deeds of Zechariah are written in the Book of the Annals of the Kings of Israel." Unfortunately, a copy of the book has never been found, so we may never learn about all of Zechariah's deeds recorded so faithfully by his scribes. The Bible mentions other missing books, too.

The **PAPYRUS LANSING** is a letter written in the 19th century B.C.E. by the royal scribe Nebmare-nakht to his young apprentice. **He praises being an Egyptian scribe as the best possible job.**

DID YOU KNOW?

ASSYRIOLOGISTS—experts who study Assyria—believe that the Assyrian king **SENNACHERIB made Nineveh the capital of Assyria** and one of the most beautiful cities of the ancient world. **He built a wall with 15 GATES around the city.** He oversaw the digging of **canals, irrigation ditches, and aqueducts**—bridge-like structures that carry water. He built an **80-ROOM PALACE** and created **gardens, parks, and temples.** Recently, the experts have suggested that **the Hanging Gardens,** one of the Seven Wonders of the Ancient World, **may have been in Nineveh,** not Babylon as they'd thought.

JONAH 1–4

JONAH TRIES TO RUN FROM GOD

One of a prophet's duties was to relay God's warnings to individuals, kings, and sometimes towns. God spoke to the Prophet Jonah about the Assyrian city Nineveh. Nineveh had fallen into wicked ways, and God wanted Jonah to let its people know God was not pleased.

Traveling into Assyrian territory was dangerous. War was a way of life for the Assyrians. They had developed nightmarish weapons and seemed to enjoy using them. Instead of facing these terrifying people, Jonah boarded a ship going in the opposite direction. He fled to Tarshish—disobeying God's command.

Angry, God hurled hurricane winds that raised giant waves. Jonah's ship shuddered and groaned as it rode waves that had turned into walls of water. The frightened sailors flung cargo overboard trying to lighten the ship's load and keep it afloat.

"This must be the work of the gods," one sailor shouted.

"But whose god?"

The men drew lots—like drawing straws—to find out who to blame, and Jonah lost. The sailors figured he was the culprit. "What have you done to make your god so angry?" they cried.

Jonah told them he had disobeyed God's orders. "Throw me into the sea," he said. "It's the only way to stop the storm."

The sailors were reluctant to kill Jonah, but they had no choice. They tossed Jonah into the sea. The water closed over his head, and he sank to the bottom. Just as Jonah's life was ebbing away, God sent a big fish that swallowed Jonah whole. Jonah lived in the belly of the fish for three days and three nights until God commanded the fish to spit Jonah out onto dry land.

The next time God told Jonah to go to Nineveh, Jonah did as he was told.

In this 1860 C.E. print by James Hagger, Jonah is spit out onto dry land by the fish that swallowed him.

THE MYSTERY OF THE LOST ARK

The Ark of the Covenant, the chest designed to hold the two stone tablets inscribed with the Ten Commandments, is one of the most sacred objects in the Bible. The Bible says it was made from acacia wood, plated with gold inside and out, and sealed with a solid gold lid. Cherubim on each end of the lid faced one another, their wings spread over the chest protectively. In the Bible, because no one was allowed to touch the ark, poles slid through rings in each corner so that priests could carry it without actually touching it. As the priests carried the ark, the Israelites followed them through the desert.

The Israelites believed the ark could not be captured or destroyed, and they carried it into battle. The Philistine soldiers were terrified by stories of the ark's power, but still they defeated the Israelites and captured it.

A model of the Ark of the Covenant is carried through Addis Ababa, Ethiopia, to the music of stringed *begenas*.

In the first Book of Samuel, the Philistines brought the ark to the Temple of Dagon in Ashdod. The next morning, the priests found the statue of their god Dagon face down before the ark. The priests set up the statue, but the next morning it was down again, this time headless and with its hands broken off. At the same time, the people of Ashdod were developing tumors. The Philistines decided to return the ark to the Israelites.

King Solomon built his great Temple in Jerusalem to hold the ark. It remained there for the Israelites to honor from 960 B.C.E. until the Babylonian empire conquered Jerusalem and destroyed the Temple in 586 B.C.E. The ark was never listed among the artifacts the Babylonians captured. Some people assumed that the ark had been destroyed along with the Temple. Others thought it may have been moved before the Babylonians attacked. The Bible later mentions that the Prophet Jeremiah hid the ark in a cave. If it had been saved, where did it go?

One theory says that for 3,000 years the ark has been protected in a church in Ethiopia, looked after by a single monk known only as the "guardian of the ark." No one but he is allowed to see it. Once a guardian has been chosen, he can never leave the church grounds again.

Another theory is that the ark never left Solomon's Temple and was instead carried through passages beneath it before the Babylonians destroyed the temple. At the end of one of the passages, it was laid to rest in the Well of Souls, a secret underground cave. Today the site of Solomon's Temple is covered by the Dome of the Rock, a Muslim shrine, on the Temple Mount.

Neither of these theories can be proved because no one is allowed to see if the Ark of the Covenant is in Ethiopia, and no one will dig beneath the Dome of the Rock because it is a sacred site. The mystery remains.

PHILISTIA, the land of the Philistines, was made up of **five city-states along the coastal plain**—Ashdod, Ashkelon, Gaza, Gath, and Ekron—each with its own **KING AND TEMPLE.**

detail from "Joshua Passing the River Jordan With the Ark of the Covenant," by Benjamin West, 1800 C.E.

DAVID THE GIANT KILLER

In the 11th century B.C.E., the Philistines—bitter enemies of the Israelites—wanted to weaken the Israelite kingdom by capturing an important mountain ridge near Bethlehem.

The Philistine army set up camp near the ridge, on the south side of the Valley of Elah. The Israelites set up camp opposite them. Neither army wanted to attack first. Finally, the Philistines decided the battle should be one Philistine champion against one Israelite champion. The Philistines sent Goliath.

Led by a shield carrier, Goliath lumbered out for all to see. He stood nearly ten feet (3 m) tall, wore a bronze helmet and full body armor, and carried a sword, spear, and javelin. "Give me a man," Goliath bellowed, "that we may fight."

For 40 days, no one accepted Goliath's dare, until a shepherd named David heard of the challenge. The Israelites' King Saul tried to discourage David, who was young and not nearly as tall and strong as Goliath. But David reminded the king that he protected his sheep from lions and bears with his slingshot. Goliath was no more dangerous. King Saul at last agreed and insisted that David wear his royal armor for protection. But the armor was too big and clunky for the boy. He shrugged it off, happier to move easily.

When Goliath made the first move toward the line of battle, David rushed toward him, whipping his sling around as he ran. When he released the stone, it shot through the air, striking Goliath in the forehead. The giant fell like a tree.

With Goliath unconscious on the ground, David pulled the giant's massive sword from its sheath, killed Goliath, and cut off his head. Their champion dead, the Philistines fled. David took Goliath's head and armor as trophies for the triumphant Israelites.

DID YOU KNOW?

In biblical times, armies had THREE types of warriors: CAVALRYMEN, who attacked from horseback or chariots; INFANTRYMEN, who carried long pikes and wore heavy armor against the chariot charges; and ARTILLERYMEN, who shot arrows and slung stones from a distance. THE STONE SLINGERS WERE THE DEADLIEST OF THEM ALL. A BALLISTICS—or firearms—expert studied the speed and accuracy of stones hurled by slings and found them equivalent to the fatal force of today's handguns. The infantryman GOLIATH, weighed down from his heavy protective armor and weapons for hand-to-hand combat, never had a chance against the stone slinger David.

David slings a stone at the giant Goliath in this 1968 C.E. lithograph by Gino D'Achille.

DISCOVERY IN THE VALLEY OF ELAH

Flanked by the gently rolling hills of Judea, the lush Valley of Elah seems too peaceful a place for an epic biblical battle. And yet this could be the site of the biblical account of the boy David, the future king of Israel, stepping forward to face the giant Philistine warrior, Goliath.

From 2007 to 2013, archaeologist Yosef Garfinkel from the Hebrew University of Jerusalem led an excavation that unearthed a 3,000-year-old fortified city overlooking the Valley of Elah. The site, called Khirbet Qeiyafa, is located on what was a main road to Jerusalem. Garfinkel wrote that the area was similar to the place described in the biblical story of David and Goliath and said that the land "was a hostile border area, where the Kingdoms of Gath and Jerusalem had constant military conflicts."

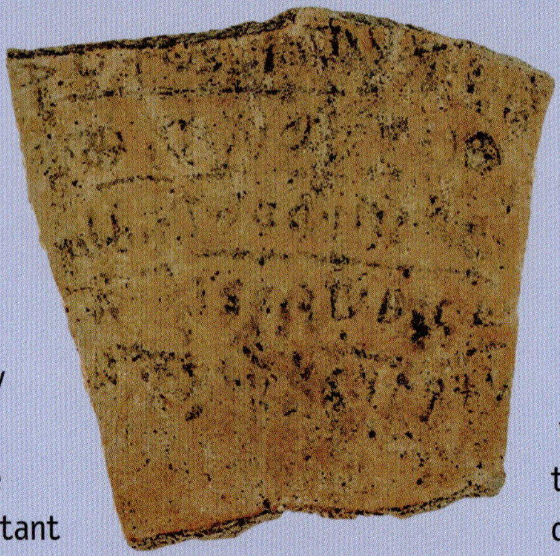

The Khirbet Qeiyafa ostracon has the oldest known Hebrew writing, about 1000 B.C.E.

The fortress at Khirbet Qeiyafa was made up of a lower city and an upper city, surrounded by a defensive wall as high as 13 feet (4 m) in places. Inside the cities, scientists have found hundreds of broken pots, stone tools, and metal objects scattered over the floors of the houses they have excavated. The mess suggests that the city was abandoned suddenly, possibly so citizens could escape a major battle. If the residents of the fortress had merely moved on to another location, they would have taken along their possessions rather than leaving them behind.

One of these broken pots, or potsherds, turned out to be the most exciting find at Khirbet Qeiyafa. This potsherd is only slightly larger than your hand, has five lines written in ink, and is thousands of years old. Scientists call a potsherd that has writing on it an ostracon. Ostracons are usually pieces broken from a vase or other earthenware object, with writing added after the piece was broken.

A 17-year-old volunteer, Oded Yair, found a potsherd on the floor of the room where he was working during the summer of 2008. He put it in a bucket along with the other potsherds he had found that morning.

That afternoon, the volunteers soaked their finds in water before carefully washing them off. It was then that they noticed the writing. Immediately, they called Khirbet Qeiyafa's expert on conservation and restoration, who told them to place the ostracon on tissue paper and let it dry slowly. When it was dry, the staff photographed the ostracon from every angle. They grew increasingly excited. There were five rows of writing. Each row of writing was separated by a black line. David Willner, an expert in Jewish antiquities, said, "To find any text is really off the charts . . . to find five lines of text is extraordinary."

After many language experts around the world examined the artifact, they agreed that the text calls for the care of slaves, orphans, widows, and strangers. There are different opinions as to what language was used and what exactly the text says. Scientists will continue to study this ostracon that dates back many centuries to help give us a better idea of what life was like in this time and place.

Scientists determined THE AGE OF TWO BURNED OLIVE PITS AT KHIRBET QEIYAFA through a process called **radiocarbon dating.** The age of the pits told them that the site had been occupied BETWEEN 1050 AND 970 B.C.E.

Some researchers believe that this wall at Khirbet Qeiyafa belonged to a palace King David built long after he defeated Goliath.

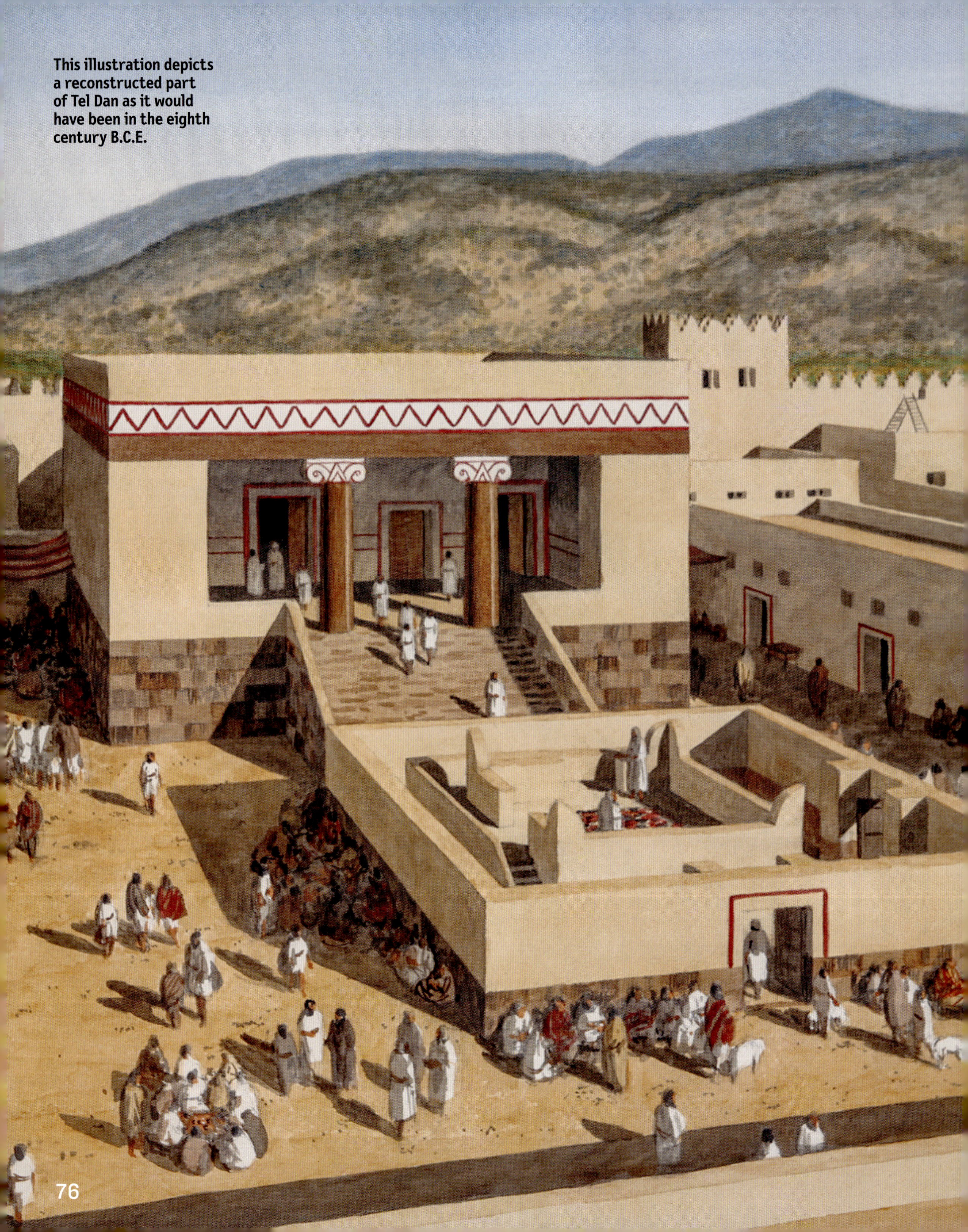

This illustration depicts a reconstructed part of Tel Dan as it would have been in the eighth century B.C.E.

THE SECRETS OF TEL DAN

A fertile piece of land, plenty of cold spring water, and a location right on the caravan route between Egypt and Syria—what better place to settle? People had been living in these foothills of Mount Hermon, in today's Israel, for thousands of years when the Canaanites moved in 5,000 years ago. They built a city named Laish. But they later lost it.

The tribe of Dan had been forced from their homeland in central Israel by the invading Philistines. The Book of Judges tells how the homeless Danites sent five spies to find a new place to live. In Laish, the spies found quiet and unsuspecting people "possessing great wealth." So an army of 600 Danites marched to Laish, killed the Canaanites, and burned down the city. The Danites built a new city called Dan.

Carved into the Tel Dan stela are words referring to the kingdom of Israel and the House of David.

Archaeologists working on this ancient site, Tel Dan, have unearthed thousands of relics that tell the story of this place. Three thousand years ago, travelers and traders passed through a series of gates in the city walls and then followed cobblestone streets to the heart of Dan. The innermost gates held rooms that could have served as guard stations in times of conflict or as market areas for artisans and tradesmen in times of peace.

Just inside the main gate, archaeologists uncovered elevated platforms. The platforms are similar to what the Bible describes as thrones at the city gates where judges, and even kings, held court over complaints and injustices.

While excavating the city walls and courtyards, archaeologists found pieces of pottery inscribed in Phoenician script and in Hebrew script, often with a name claiming ownership of the pot. The most exciting find was an inscription chiseled in Aramaic on basalt stone. The inscribed fragments were once part of a stone monument, or stela. The text, written in the ninth century B.C.E., boasts of a victory over two kings—"the king of Israel" and the "king of the House of David." This inscription is special because it is the only nonbiblical reference to King David ever found.

Even earlier, sometime in the 18th century B.C.E., the Canaanites built an enormous mud-brick gate consisting of three elegant arches. Archaeologists found this archway still intact. Until this discovery, historians believed the Romans had invented the arch. But the Canaanite archway is nearly 4,000 years old, predating the first Roman arch by 1,500 years.

The second Book of Kings tells the story of battles fought over the control of this strategic city. Just as fortifications built by the Canaanites eventually failed to protect Laish, so the impressive fortifications of the Danites failed to protect Dan. The Assyrians invaded in the eighth century B.C.E. and destroyed the city.

Outside the gates of Dan, archaeologists unearthed **A BENCH.** The Bible tells of **elders sitting outside the gatehouse** to hear news from the outside world, share gossip, and rest against the city wall.

DID YOU KNOW?

THE QUEEN OF SHEBA is the **first foreign queen mentioned specifically in the Bible,** and yet her name, unlike later queens Esther or Jezebel, is not mentioned. The majority of queens did not actually rule as the Queen of Sheba did but were referred to by the Aramaic word *shegal*, which means **"KING'S WIFE."**

"The Judgment of Solomon," by Francesco Podesti, about 1836 C.E.

I KINGS 3

THE WISDOM OF SOLOMON

Solomon was just a boy when he became king. Soon God appeared to him in a dream and offered to grant him a wish. Solomon, concerned about his youth and inexperience, asked God for wisdom to govern such a large and great nation.

God was pleased that the young ruler had not asked for glory in battle, a long life, or riches. He bestowed Solomon not only with wisdom but also with all those things Solomon had not asked for—honor and wealth like no other king had ever had.

Solomon's first test followed soon after this dream. Two women appeared before him. The first woman explained to Solomon that she lived in the same house as the second woman. They had both given birth to sons within three days of one another. The second woman had rolled over on her son in the middle of the night and smothered him. So she switched babies, leaving her dead son next to the first woman and stealing the first woman's son.

"No," the second woman cried out in denial to the first woman. "The living son is mine; yours is dead."

"No," the first woman replied. "The living son is mine."

Finally, Solomon called for his sword. He ordered, "Cut the baby in two and give each of them half."

Horrified, the first woman begged Solomon, "Don't kill him. Give the baby to her, but don't hurt him."

The second woman cried, "Divide the child in half."

Solomon spoke, "The real mother would give up her son rather than see him killed. Give the child to her."

News of the verdict spread far and wide, and the people knew that God had given Solomon the great gift of wisdom.

DIGGING FOR PALACE TREASURES

Jet-lagged and exhausted, archaeologist Eric Cline and his team stumbled onto the bus. They stifled yawns as the bus lumbered past avocado and banana plantations in the western Galilee region of Israel. All weariness evaporated a few minutes later when the bus lurched to a stop at the Tel Kabri archaeological site. This was the first morning of the 2013 digging season at the site, which dates back to around 1700 B.C.E., and no one knew exactly what to expect. The moon, low in the sky, gave a beautiful glow to the site. The remains of ancient walls outlined a palace complex of the Canaanites—the largest in northern Israel. What story would the remains tell about royal life 3,700 years ago?

The team prepared the site for excavation. As the days passed, they uncovered pieces of pottery and other finds, carefully using tools that would keep the pieces intact. Cline described the process as "controlled destruction" where every detail is recorded and photographed—even changes in the color of the dirt. This data is then available for future scientists to study.

In July, while excavating just west of the palace's central courtyard, the team discovered an enclosed room buried under debris of mud bricks and plaster. Further investigation revealed that this 15-by-25-foot (4.5-by-7.5-m) enclosure was a storeroom. After uncovering 40 three-foot (1-m)-tall ceramic jars, they suspected that they had found a wine cellar—the oldest and largest found to date. This room stood close to a ceremonial hall, where kings may have held banquets for royalty from near and far. Imagine guests dining on finely prepared goat while servants fetched wine from the wine cellar. The cellar likely held the equivalent of 3,000 bottles of red and white wine.

In the palace complex at Tel Kabri, archaeologists discovered these ceramic jars in a wine cellar.

The Bible mentions wine and winemaking hundreds of times. When rainfall was scarce, wine was safer to drink than the muddy, polluted water at the bottom of a well. The Book of Nehemiah describes wine storehouses such as this one at Tel Kabri. Other ancient texts also reveal the importance of wine production in the biblical lands. Winemaking recipes were recorded in the Mari texts from 18th century B.C.E. Mesopotamia and the Ebers Papyrus from 16th century B.C.E. Egypt. Experts tested remains from inside the jars discovered in Tel Kabri's cellar and found the same ingredients as in these ancient recipes—including honey, mint, cinnamon bark, and juniper berries.

As the 2013 digging season came to an end, the archaeologists closed up the site for safekeeping until the next season. Cline's team took their last predawn bus ride to the excavation. Accustomed now to the 4:30 a.m. workday starts, they were no longer weary; instead, they were energized by the secrets the tel had revealed to them—and curious about those it still held.

At Tel Megiddo, in Israel, recent excavations may have uncovered **KING AHAB'S STABLES** from the ninth century B.C.E. Nearby structures could have held **the king's battle chariots.**

entrance to the royal palace in the ancient city of Ugarit

HEZEKIAH THE FAITHFUL

After Solomon's death, the kingdom of the Israelites split in two: Israel and Judah. Eventually, Israel was destroyed by the Assyrians and its people scattered. Judah, under King Ahaz, had fallen into evil ways. Ahaz had neglected the Temple and worshipped idols. When his son Hezekiah came to the throne at only 25 years of age, the new king knew that Judah would be destroyed like Israel unless the people changed their ways and became faithful to God.

Hezekiah was determined to stop all idol worship, so he destroyed the false idols and removed the elevated areas of land where they were worshipped. God rewarded Hezekiah. Judah prospered along with its king. Battles against the Philistines ended in victory. Storehouses bulged with grain, wine, and oil.

But in the 14th year of Hezekiah's reign, the Assyrian king Sennacherib invaded Judah. He conquered one city after another.

In Jerusalem, Hezekiah armed his people with weapons and shields, and then he gathered them in the courtyard by the city gate. "Be strong," he told them. "God is on our side."

Sennacherib surrounded Jerusalem and sent a letter to Hezekiah saying that Jerusalem would fall like all the cities before it. He said that no god would save Hezekiah—he must surrender.

At first, Hezekiah tried to pay for a peace agreement. He gave Sennacherib all the silver and gold in the Temple and treasuries and even the gold that adorned the Temple doors and doorposts. But Sennacherib continued his threats. Finally, God lashed out, sending an angel who killed 185,000 of Sennacherib's men and forced him to retreat and return home.

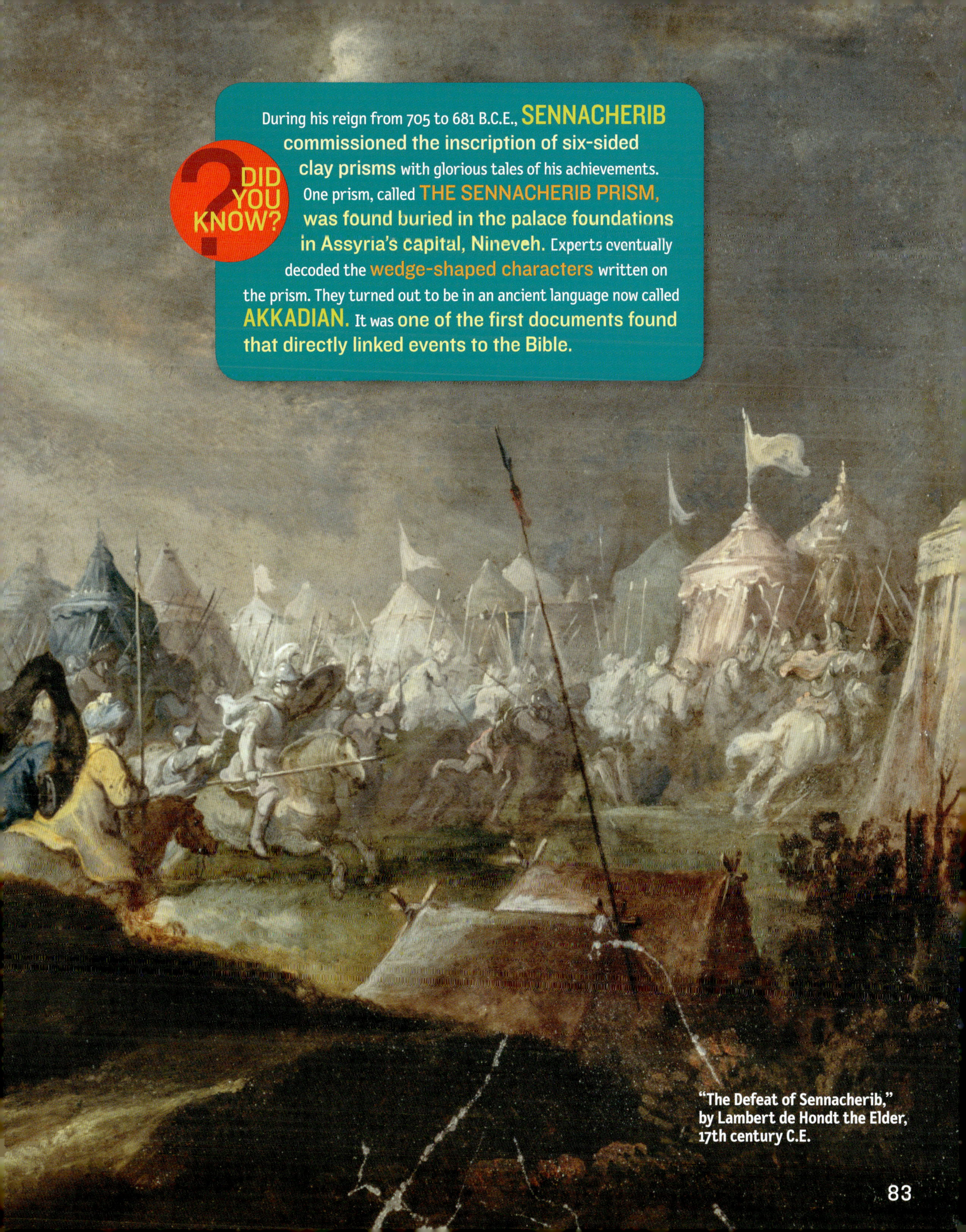

DID YOU KNOW?

During his reign from 705 to 681 B.C.E., **SENNACHERIB** commissioned the inscription of six-sided clay prisms with glorious tales of his achievements. One prism, called **THE SENNACHERIB PRISM,** was found buried in the palace foundations in Assyria's capital, Nineveh. Experts eventually decoded the wedge-shaped characters written on the prism. They turned out to be in an ancient language now called **AKKADIAN.** It was one of the first documents found that directly linked events to the Bible.

"The Defeat of Sennacherib," by Lambert de Hondt the Elder, 17th century C.E.

an aerial view of the ruins of the Herodium, Herod's great palace-fortress, a few miles south of Jerusalem

HERODʼS GREAT HOUSES

Herod the Great was made king of Judea (territory encompassing the southern part of ancient Israel) by the Romans around 40 B.C.E. He was a feared tyrant, but he was a great builder. During his reign, he built at least 11 great fortresses.

Archaeologists have restored many of the ancient buildings at Herod's fortress Masada, constructed on a huge rock plateau at the eastern edge of the Judean Desert. Herod turned Masada into a fortified hideout between 37 and 31 B.C.E. To show that he was master over everything—even the desert—Herod installed bathhouses that required plentiful water. In the dry desert, water had to be channeled from nearby oases; then it was held in big containers, or cisterns, at the bottom of the plateau. Slaves carted water up the plateau when it was needed. The baths were heated, which meant wood had to be hauled from forests far away.

Herod built Roman-style bathhouses in all of his buildings, each typically including a changing room, a warm room for relaxing, a hot steam room, and a cold-water plunge pool. The garden pool was larger than two Olympic-size swimming pools.

The only project Herod chose to name after himself—the mountain complex of Herodium—may have been where he was buried. First, Herod built a mountain high enough to overlook the entire region around Jerusalem. Next, at the top, he built a strong palace-fort. At the bottom, he built a small town. Roman aqueducts, or bridges designed to carry water aboveground, were built to channel water from faraway springs into a pool for the people in lower Herodium. Cisterns in lower Herodium held rainwater to supply upper Herodium.

detail of “Herod and Herodias at the Feast of Herod,” by Frans Francken the Younger, 16th century C.E.

To flatter the Romans who had made him king of Judea, Herod built the city of Caesarea honoring the emperor Augustus Caesar. It boasts one of the world's first man-made harbors. The harbor's seawalls unexpectedly created waves that deposited a wide strip of sand along the shore. Herod turned this sandbar into a stadium for chariot racing.

Herod knew that so much Roman architecture, and especially the foreign pagan practices, offended his Jewish subjects. The Jews also resented being taxed by Roman laws. To try to satisfy them, Herod rebuilt Jerusalem and expanded the Temple complex first built by King Solomon.

First, Herod enlarged the Temple Mount and on top created a platform bigger than 24 football fields. To help support the platform, he built huge arched vaults beneath the mountain. Archaeologists have calculated that some stones in the arches weighed 550 tons (499 t) or more. The project continued after Herod's death in 4 B.C.E. and was still under way around 30 C.E. when Jesus and his disciples visited the Temple for Passover. The Temple was destroyed by Romans in 70 C.E. Today, only its Western Wall stands. Jews from all over the world visit the site to pray.

Herod expanded **Jerusalem's largest public bath, THE SILOAM POOL,** where the faithful cleansed before entering the Temple. The Gospel of John (9:1–11) says **Jesus healed the blind man** at this pool.

PART II NEW TESTAMENT: THE WORLD OF JESUS

Four hundred years after the Old Testament ends, the New Testament begins. While the Old Testament covers 1,000 years of history, the New Testament covers only 50 to 75 years. But it is filled with drama: Jesus the Messiah ("the chosen one") is born, miracles are performed, and Jesus' message is spread by his apostles. Finally, there is a vision of an apocalypse—the end of the world—and the battle between good and evil.

Many people believe that the books of the New Testament were written to be read during church services to give people moral guidance. In the second century C.E., the stories were collected into one book. In 397 C.E., it became the New Testament.

In this section, we retell the stories of the life and teachings of Jesus, from his birth to his death and resurrection. You'll follow Jesus from town to town as he preaches about the kingdom of God and as he tends to the poor and heals the sick.

You'll also join archaeologists who uncover pieces of this ancient world, from the "Jesus boat" at the murky bottom of the Sea of Galilee to mysterious symbols that identified secret Christian meeting places. Fascinating facts tie the stories and archaeology together and bring the New Testament to life.

"For in Christ Jesus, you are all CHILDREN OF GOD through FAITH."
—GALATIANS 3:26

"Entry of the Christ in Jerusalem," by Jean-Léon Gérôme, 1897 C.E.

LUKE 2:1–20

THE BIRTH OF JESUS

It had been a long journey—nearly 100 miles (160 km) from Nazareth to Bethlehem. Joseph had walked, leading a donkey that carried his wife, Mary. The Roman emperor Caesar Augustus had ordered a census. Everyone had to return to their ancestral home to be counted. Joseph and Mary's lineage reached back to King David, requiring them to travel to David's hometown of Bethlehem. It was a hard trip for Mary, who was about to give birth.

With so many arriving for the census, Bethlehem's guest rooms had already been filled by the time they arrived. Mary needed a place to have her baby, so she and Joseph settled into a room where animals were kept. It was quiet, and the straw made a soft bed.

After the birth, Mary wrapped her newborn baby, named Jesus, in strips of cloth and made him comfortable in a manger—a feeding trough for animals. Meanwhile, an angel appeared to shepherds watching over their sheep in the nearby hills and announced the birth.

"I bring good news," the angel said, and then the angel told the shepherds where to find Jesus in a manger: "To you is born this day in the city of David a Savior, who is the Messiah." Suddenly the sky was filled with angels praising God.

After the angels returned to heaven, the shepherds quickly made their way to Bethlehem to find the baby.

The shepherds found the baby Jesus just as the angel had described. They fell to their knees and told how the angels appeared to them in the hills. Mary listened in amazement. Silently, she pondered the angel's words—"savior," "messiah." Her heart swelled, as she treasured each word. It was indeed, "good news of great joy for all the people."

"The Adoration of the Shepherds," by Giorgione, 1505–10 C.E.

DID YOU KNOW?

The Book of Matthew does not tell us how many **WISE MEN,** or magi, came from the East to pay tribute to Jesus. The tradition of **THREE** comes from the number of **GIFTS** offered to Jesus. These three gifts also were highly valuable and given to a king or deity as an offering. **GOLD** is a precious metal. **FRANKINCENSE** is an aromatic resin, a kind of oil, used as incense in worship and as a remedy for pain. And **MYRRH** is used to anoint, or bless, someone or to embalm the dead.

A silver star on the floor of the Grotto of the Nativity, under the Church of the Nativity in Bethlehem, marks the spot traditionally believed to be where Jesus was born.

THE CHURCH OF THE NATIVITY

Helena, the Roman emperor Constantine's mother, embraced Christianity with fervor. In 327 C.E., she traveled from Rome to Judea, determined to find the sites where the stories about Jesus had taken place. Helena said she identified Joseph's carpentry shop, the field where the angel appeared to the shepherds announcing the arrival of the Messiah, the spot where Jesus performed the miracle of seven loaves and fishes, and also the stump of the tree from which Jesus' cross had been cut. Helena's pilgrimage marked holy sites like a string of pearls throughout Judea. The precise locations that Helena indicated have been accepted in Christian tradition.

To mark the holy sites, Helena and Constantine built churches and shrines. One of the most sacred sites on which Helena built was a cave in Bethlehem traditionally believed to be where Mary gave birth to Jesus. Helena and Constantine commissioned a church to be built directly over the cave. Although the Bible doesn't mention if Jesus was born in a cave, it was not uncommon for houses at the time to be built in front of caves. The cave itself would be used as a stable and would likely contain a feeding trough, or manger.

Detail from a painting depicting the birth of Jesus, by Bernardinus Indisur, in San Bernardino Church, Verona, Italy

Helena's eight-sided Church of the Nativity was completed around 337 C.E. In the center of the church, a hole in the floor afforded a view down into the cave to the very spot Helena indicated Mary gave birth. Although some of the floor mosaics survive from this first church, most of the church burned to the ground in the sixth century C.E.

The Byzantine emperor Justinian rebuilt the church in 565 C.E. Bigger and grander, the church now looked more like a fortress. It was sturdy, too. This second Church of the Nativity has survived invasions, rebellions, sieges, earthquakes, and fires. It is the church that stands there today.

While most churches in the Holy Land were destroyed during the Persian invasion in 614 C.E., according to legend the Church of the Nativity was spared because of a mosaic of the three wise men, or magi. The magi were dressed in Persian clothing, and the commander of the Persian army was so moved by this that he ordered his soldiers not to touch the church.

The main entrance to the church is low, forcing people to bend down when entering. It is appropriately called the Door of Humility. There are many theories as to why the doorway was designed this way. Some say it was to prevent thieves from bringing in wagons to cart away their loot. Others say it was to keep even the most noble person from entering on horseback.

In the web of caverns below the church, one dimly lit rectangular cave is where Helena marked Jesus' birthplace. Marking the exact spot on the marble floor of the cave is a 14-pointed star inscribed with the Latin phrase *"Hic de Virgine Maria Jesus Christus natus est*—Here Jesus Christ was born to the Virgin Mary."

In the Gospel of Matthew, **JESUS' GENEALOGY,** or family tree, **has three groups of 14 ancestors.** The silver star on the cave floor beneath the Church of the Nativity has **14 POINTS TO SYMBOLIZE THEM.**

LUKE 2:39–52

THE BOY JESUS IN THE TEMPLE

Jesus was 12 years old and living in a little village called Nazareth. With friends and family he had made the annual pilgrimage to Jerusalem to celebrate Passover. Passover is one of three important pilgrim festivals for Jews, along with the Feast of Weeks and the Feast of Tabernacles. Passover commemorates the Israelites' freedom from slavery and God's protection of their firstborn sons.

After a week of celebrations, the festival ended and Mary and Joseph headed home. They both assumed Jesus was traveling with another family member. After a day, Jesus was nowhere to be found. Mary and Joseph raced back to Jerusalem. They searched the city but could not find him.

Finally, on the third day, they found Jesus at the Temple among the religious elders. The Temple, built by Solomon and later rebuilt by Herod, was a gathering place for worship and learning. In the middle of one group was Jesus, discussing Jewish law with men much older than he was. Mary and Joseph watched Jesus listening, asking questions, and offering answers. Everyone was amazed at the young boy's wisdom.

Mary's relief at finding Jesus turned to annoyance. She scolded, "Why have you treated us like this? Your father and I have been frantically looking for you."

"Why were you searching for me?" Jesus calmly asked his mother. "Didn't you know that I had to be in my Father's house?"

Mary and Joseph were confused. What had Jesus meant by that?

In Nazareth, Jesus again became the obedient son. His mother forgave him and treasured all he had said.

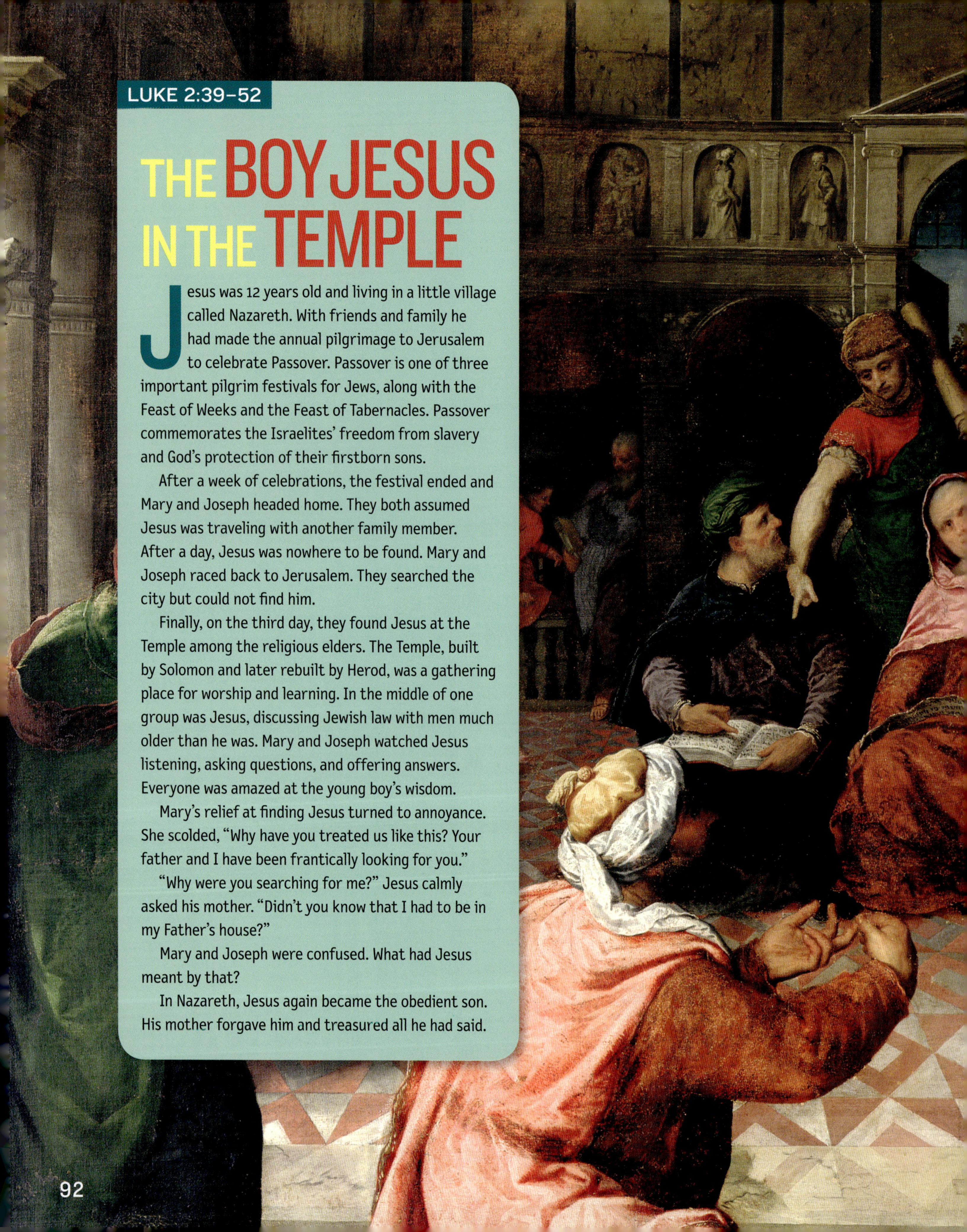

DID YOU KNOW?

During **FESTIVALS,** pilgrims would have **SMELLED** Jerusalem long before they reached it. Fires burned day and night. The smell of woodsmoke mingled with the distinct odor of burning meat as whole animals were sacrificed on the Temple's altar. In the Jewish Bible, **THE BOOK OF NUMBERS,** chapter 28, lays out the schedule for daily, monthly, and special occasion burnt animal offerings. **DURING PASSOVER,** when Jesus was discussing Jewish law with the Temple elders, priests ceremoniously burned two young bulls, one ram, and seven male lambs.

detail from "Christ Disputing in the Temple," by Paris Bordone, about 1545 C.E.

detail from "The Baptism of Christ," by Nicolas Poussin, about 1658 C.E.

DID YOU KNOW?

THE GOSPELS, which may have been written in the second half of the first century C.E., are stories about Jesus' birth, life, ministry, and death. Four Gospels are included in the New Testament—**MATTHEW, MARK, LUKE, AND JOHN.** Matthew, Mark, and Luke's accounts focus on Jesus' **HUMANNESS** during his last year of ministry. They are so similar they are known as the Synoptic Gospels, meaning they should be read together (*synoptikos* means "seen together" in Greek). John emphasizes Jesus' **GODLINESS** over all three to four years of his ministry.

MATTHEW 3

JOHN THE BAPTIST AT THE RIVER JORDAN

John the Baptist chose to live in the Wilderness of Judea, far from the corruption of Jerusalem. He preached on the banks of the River Jordan, attracting large crowds. His clothes were made from camel's hair, tied at the waist with a leather belt. He ate locusts and wild honey. His message was simple: "Repent, the Lord is coming!"

In the waters of the Jordan, John baptized those who came to him confessing their sins. Baptism is a religious rite where a person is immersed in water, symbolically washing away his sins. It didn't matter to John who you were or where you came from as long as you were repentant, telling God you were sorry for your sins. He told powerful and wealthy officials who claimed to be descendants of Abraham that a good relationship with God was more important than genealogy.

John's followers looked to him for guidance to build a good relationship with God. John told them to share with those less fortunate. "If you have two coats, share with someone who has none. If you have more food than you can eat, share with someone who is hungry." Even the tax collectors were told to take only what money was due instead of taking some extra for themselves. His followers whispered: Was John the Messiah? But John told them he wasn't worthy to even untie the true Messiah's sandals. "I baptize you with water," John told his followers. "The Messiah will baptize you with the Holy Spirit and fire."

At the beginning of his ministry, Jesus traveled from Galilee to be baptized by John. As Jesus came out of the water, the heavens opened up and the spirit of God descended in the form of a dove. A voice from heaven cried out, "This is my Son, the Beloved, with whom I am well pleased."

DID YOU KNOW?

In biblical times, **people believed that disease was caused by an EVIL SPIRIT entering, or possessing, a person.** An **EXORCISM,** a ceremony that expelled the **evil spirit,** was a common cure.

MATTHEW 4:25, 5–7

THE SERMON ON THE MOUNT

Jesus traveled throughout Galilee teaching in synagogues and healing the sick. Soon crowds appeared wherever Jesus went. Everyone was anxious for his healing touch.

One day Jesus looked out over the crowd and saw people who had come from Syria, Galilee, Decapolis, Jerusalem, Judea, and beyond to be healed. He climbed a nearby mountain and sat down. People gathered around him to listen to his sermon.

Jesus explained how virtues in life would ultimately be rewarded. The humble, the meek, those who mourn—all have reason to be happy because they will be welcomed by God. The peacemakers, the merciful, the pure of heart will all be rewarded for their faithfulness. His followers would suffer hardships and challenges, but they, too, would be rewarded in heaven.

Next, Jesus told the people that the law of the Old Testament should always be followed. Obeying God's law meant teaching others by example. But it wasn't enough to follow the law in their actions; they must also follow the law in their hearts and minds. They must not hold anger. They must love their enemies. For all of this, they would be rewarded in heaven.

Jesus told his listeners that they should follow God's laws for the right reasons. Those who pray, fast, or give to charity just so that others will notice will not receive any future rewards. God appreciates the pure of heart, who conduct themselves simply and privately in God's name.

Jesus told the crowd how to pray by teaching them the Lord's Prayer. Then he ended the sermon with a parable—a story that teaches a lesson. He said that those who heard the sermon and did not follow his advice were as foolish as the man who builds his house on unstable sand. Those who heard his words and followed them were as wise as the man who builds his house on solid rock.

Jesus speaks to the crowds in this depiction of the Sermon on the Mount by Joos de Momper (1564–1635).

fisherman fishing
in the Sea of Galilee

THE BOAT OF GALILEE

During 1985–86, a dry spell affected the Sea of Galilee, the body of water along whose shores the Bible says Jesus preached and performed miracles. Actually a freshwater lake, Galilee's water level fell so low that the areas along the shore dried into mudflats. People were alarmed to see their main water supply drying up. But two brothers saw this as an opportunity. They were amateur archaeologists who dreamed of discovering an ancient ship. This was the perfect time to search for one at the bottom of the Sea of Galilee.

Skilled archaeologists would have told them that the search was useless. Wood decays rapidly in warm freshwater. If a boat had sunk in ancient times in the Sea of Galilee, nothing would be left of it. The brothers didn't know any better. They went boat hunting. After days of turning up coins, bits of metal, and nails, they spied a faint curve of wood in the mud. It was a plank from the frame of an ancient boat.

Israel's Department of Antiquities verified that the plank indeed belonged to an ancient fishing boat that had been preserved by tightly packed mud. Then experts got involved. They had to remove the boat from the mud without damaging it before water levels rose back to normal. Scientists worked around the clock. They suspended platforms over the boat so they could work without stepping on it. Lying on their bellies on the platforms, the archaeologists hovered over the boat and dug the mud out of the hull. Once the wood was exposed to air it had to be kept wet to prevent it from shrinking and warping. Volunteers sprayed the wood night and day for almost two weeks while the boat was being excavated.

Once all the mud had been cleared out, the hull was reinforced with fiberglass and then the entire boat was encased in foam. The foam not only protected the wood just as the mud had done for 2,000 years, it also allowed the boat to float. Experts could now safely move it into a specially made chemical pool where it could be restored.

Found in deep mud in the Sea of Galilee, this boat dates back to the time when Jesus was preaching.

The restoration took seven years. Before they worked on the spongy timbers, they ran tests to determine what kind of wood it was. Experts found ten different kinds, suggesting the boat had undergone many repairs or had been made out of scrap. The frame of the Galilean boat is oak, but most of the planks are made from Lebanese cedar—the same wood Solomon used to build his Temple and palace—prized for its sturdiness.

Archaeologists suspected from the hull's construction, as well as pottery and nails found with it, that the boat dated to the first century C.E. Tests supported this, so people started calling the Galilee boat the "Jesus boat" because it was found to be from the same time Jesus could have lived. Although there is no evidence that Jesus actually sailed in the boat, it's the kind Jesus and his disciples would have fished and traveled in.

After Jesus died, it was dangerous to follow his teachings. Followers used a **FISH SYMBOL** as a secret sign. When meeting a stranger, **a follower drew half a fish.** The stranger who finished it was a follower, too.

BREAD is used as a **symbol of spiritual nourishment** in many places in the Bible. After feeding thousands of people, Jesus reminded his followers that God had provided bread—called **MANNA**—to the Israelites in the desert as they fled from slavery in Egypt. He told them **it was not Moses who had provided the food, but God.** After Jesus fed the people, he said to them, **"I AM THE BREAD OF LIFE. WHOEVER COMES TO ME WILL NEVER BE HUNGRY."** He was telling them that God satisfies **spiritual needs** as well as physical hunger.

DID YOU KNOW?

detail from "The Miracle of the Loaves and Fishes," by James Tissot, 1886–96 C.E.

MATTHEW 14:13–21

FEEDING THE MULTITUDE

Jesus and his disciples were so busy teaching and healing, they had no time to rest or to reflect (think quietly and calmly). Crowds appeared everywhere, eager to hear their sermons and be healed by their touch.

In order to renew his strength and to think about all he planned to do, Jesus said to his disciples, "We must go to a deserted place."

Secretly, they boarded a boat to a remote city called Bethsaida.

But Jesus could no longer travel unrecognized, and when people saw him they ran along the shore ahead of the boat. Soon hundreds, and then thousands, followed.

When Jesus stepped off the boat, crowds of people were waiting for him. As tired as he was, he had great compassion for them. They were like sheep without a shepherd. So he set out to teach them and heal them.

When it grew late, Jesus' disciples advised him, "It's time to send these people on their way to find something to eat in the nearby villages."

Jesus told the disciples to feed the people instead.

"All we have is five loaves of barley bread and two fish," said the disciples. "There are 5,000 men alone, not counting the women and children!"

"Bring the food to me," said Jesus.

Jesus looked up to heaven and blessed the food. He broke the loaves and gave them to the disciples who handed them out to the people. Jesus divided the fish as well.

When he was done, everyone had eaten their fill.

Then the disciples gathered the leftovers: 12 baskets of barley bread and fish.

Whispers rippled through the crowd. "This must be the prophet."

DID YOU KNOW?

The Bible says that PETER GAVE UP FISHING TO FOLLOW JESUS, and Jesus told him that he was **the solid foundation—"THE ROCK"—**on which Jesus' church would be built. After Jesus died, Peter preached Jesus' message until **Peter was crucified** by the Roman emperor Nero. Tradition says that **the site of Peter's death is today's CLEMENTINE CHAPEL,** beneath the Vatican in Rome. **Catholic Church beliefs hold that Peter was their FIRST LEADER** and that today's pope follows in his footsteps.

detail from "Peter Walks on Water," by Philipp Otto Runge, 1806 C.E.

MATTHEW 14:22–33

JESUS WALKS ON WATER

After Jesus and his disciples fed the multitude with only a few loaves of barley bread and fish, Jesus sent his disciples in their boat across the Sea of Galilee, back to Capernaum. Jesus did not accompany them, but he left the crowds and climbed the mountain to pray alone.

While Jesus was praying, a storm blew in. Waves filled the sea, and wind battered the disciples' boat. The disciples struggled to pull the oars all night long.

By early morning, they had rowed only a few miles. They were still battling the wind and the waves when they saw someone walking toward them—*on top of the water.*

"It's a ghost," they cried out, terrified.

"Take heart! It is I—do not be afraid," Jesus called out to the disciples.

Peter, the bravest and most faithful, answered: "If it is you, command me to come to you."

"Come," Jesus said.

Peter climbed out of the boat. He started toward Jesus, but a gust of wind hit him and frightened him. His faith wavered when he realized he was standing on the stormy sea. Peter began to sink. "Lord, save me!" he cried.

Jesus held out his hand. "You of little faith," he said. "Why did you doubt?"

Jesus helped the soggy Peter back into the boat and then climbed in himself. The moment Jesus stepped into the boat, the wind stopped. The sea calmed. They soon reached the shore.

The disciples were stunned. When they realized the miracle they had just witnessed, they worshipped Jesus and said, "Truly you are the Son of God."

LUKE 15

THE PRODIGAL SON

Jesus often taught by telling his followers a parable, which is a story designed to teach a moral lesson. When his opponents complained that Jesus often shared his meal with sinners, Jesus explained that heaven celebrates more over one sinner who repents his sins than over 99 righteous people. He told the parable of the prodigal son as an example of this.

A "prodigal" person is one who wastes money. In this parable, the younger of two brothers demanded his inheritance from his father. His father gave it to him, and the boy packed up and traveled far away. He spent the money on foolish things and soon had nothing left. He had to take a job feeding pigs and was so hungry he wanted to eat the pigs' slop.

One day, he thought, "Here I am dying of hunger, when my father's servants eat so well, and there are always leftovers." He decided to go home and ask to be one of his father's servants.

The father saw his son walking toward him from a distance. He ran to meet the young man and joyfully embraced him. His son confessed that he had sinned against heaven and his father and was not worthy to be a son but a servant. The happy father would hear none of it. He ordered his servants to fetch his son the best coat as well as a ring and sandals. "Slaughter our fattest calf," he cried. "Let's celebrate!"

The older son, working in the fields, heard music and dancing. A servant told him, "Your brother has come home."

Furious, the older brother told his father that he had worked hard all these years and had been obedient—and there had never been a party for him!

"But, my son," the father said, "we have to celebrate, don't you understand? Your brother was lost, and now he's found!"

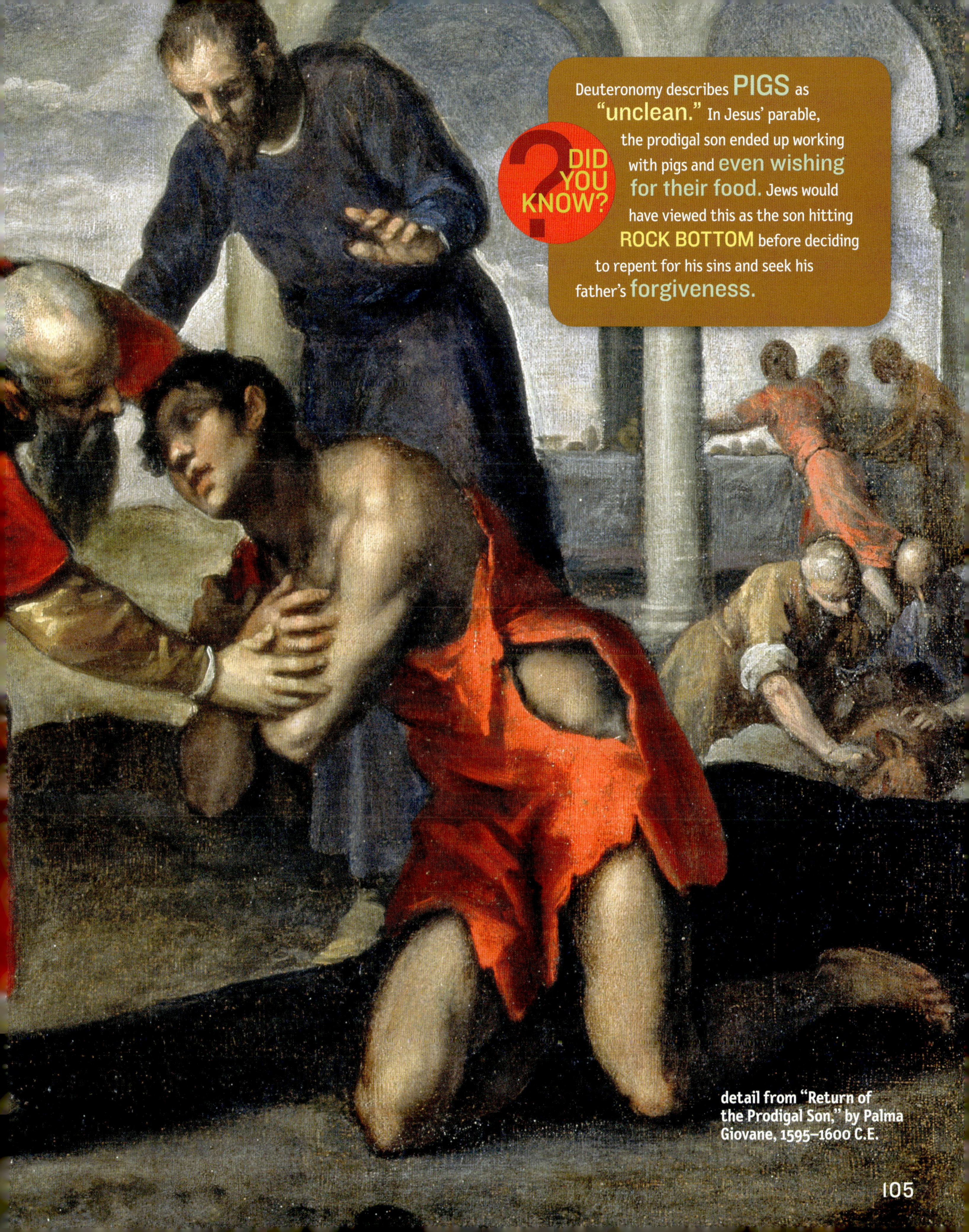

DID YOU KNOW?

Deuteronomy describes **PIGS** as **"unclean."** In Jesus' parable, the prodigal son ended up working with pigs and **even wishing for their food.** Jews would have viewed this as the son hitting **ROCK BOTTOM** before deciding to repent for his sins and seek his father's **forgiveness.**

detail from "Return of the Prodigal Son," by Palma Giovane, 1595–1600 C.E.

DID YOU KNOW?

The **variety of money** coming into towns from trading with different areas led to the job of **MONEY CHANGER.** Money changers used **benches drawn with lines and squares** for calculating. The word "bank" comes from the term *banco*, or bench. Once the money was exchanged, **coins from all across the MIDDLE EAST** were handed over to the Temple authorities to be deposited into the Temple treasury. MONEY CHANGERS COULD NOT MAKE ANY EXTRA MONEY, OR **INTEREST,** on their transactions. It was against Jewish law.

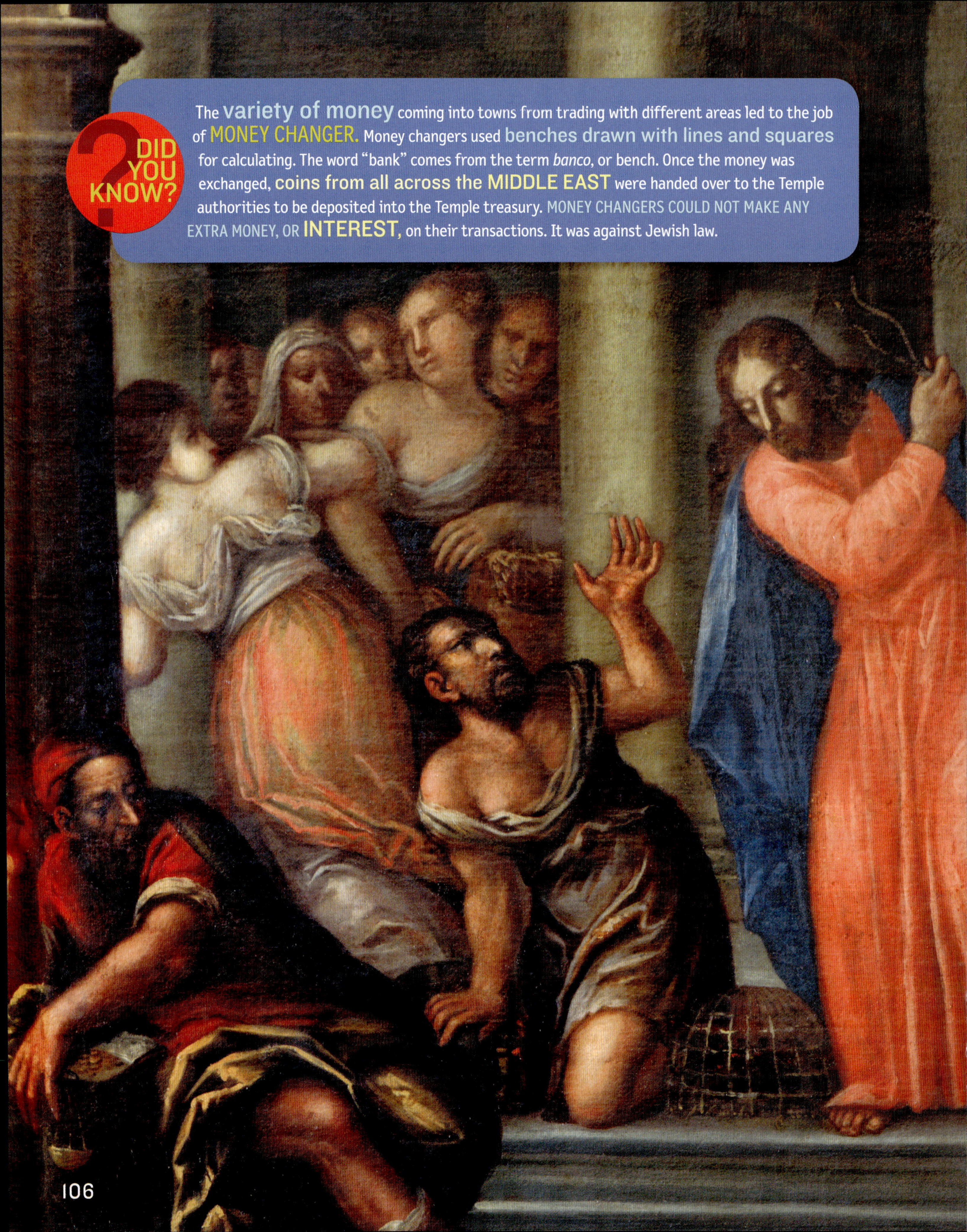

LUKE 19:28–48, MATTHEW 21:1–17, JOHN 2:13–25, MARK 11:7–19

JESUS CLEANSES THE TEMPLE

The Sunday before Jesus died, he and his disciples traveled to Jerusalem to celebrate Passover. The roads were crowded with pilgrims on their way to the annual festival. Any other king might have entered Jerusalem riding an impressive stallion. But Jesus, often called king of the Jews, chose to ride a humble donkey—the hardworking beast of the common people.

They had not gone far down the winding path from the Mount of Olives when a crowd began to form around Jesus. Those in front of the small procession spread their cloaks across the road. Others cut palm fronds and paved the road with the broad leaves. As they escorted Jesus to the city gates, they shouted, "Blessed is the king who comes in the name of the Lord!"

When Jesus passed through the gates of Jerusalem, the townspeople whispered to one another, "Who is this?"

The crowds that had followed him announced, "This is the prophet Jesus from Nazareth Galilee."

The following day, Jesus and his disciples returned to Jerusalem. They entered the great plaza at the Temple where vendors sold their goods, including cattle, sheep, and doves. Money changers sat at their tables exchanging Roman coins for Temple currency that people could use to purchase animals suitable for sacrifice. Jesus was outraged that a holy place was being used for buying and selling. He grabbed some cords to make a whip. Thrashing the whip, he drove out the traders, along with their cattle and sheep, from the Temple courtyard. He overturned the money changers' tables, scattering their coins everywhere, and cried: "Take these things out of here! Stop making my Father's house a marketplace!"

"Jesus Cleanses the Temple," in the Church of San Gaetano, Padova (Padua), Italy, by unknown 17th-century artist

TEMPLE LIFE DURING JESUS' TIME

During the time of Jesus, hundreds of thousands of pilgrims came to the Temple in Jerusalem to celebrate Passover each year. Before entering the Temple, the pilgrims would have had a ritual cleansing in one of the many baths fed by 50 miles (80.5 km) of aqueducts and pipes. Pilgrims would then enter the Double Gate on the south side of the Temple and pass through a tunnel lit by flickering candles. Above them, the tunnel ceiling was carved and painted with intricate designs much like a Persian carpet.

The tunnel opened into the Court of the Gentiles, the Temple's main courtyard that also served as a public market. Here, vendors sold lambs and doves for sacrifice. Before purchasing an animal, pilgrims would have to exchange their money for Temple currency. They could not use Roman coins, which were stamped with the head of Caesar, because coins with images of people or animals were considered an abomination to the Lord. The Temple coins were simply stamped with the words "Jerusalem the Holy."

A model of Herod's Temple based on accounts of the day is in Jerusalem's Israel Museum.

Everyone was allowed into the Court of the Gentiles, an open space the size of six football fields. Workmen had wrestled enormous stones out of a quarry and into place to form the retaining walls that supported the plaza. The largest stone was 40 feet (12 m) long and weighed 400 tons (363 t). No modern crane would be able to lift this stone. It is the largest stone in the world from a quarry.

The areas closer to the Temple were off-limits for many people. Only Jewish men and women could pass through the Beautiful Gate and climb the stairs that led to the Court of the Women. These stairs were deliberately built to be uneven. This forced pilgrims to climb slowly, with attention and reverence.

Jewish women could go only as far as the Court of the Women. Here, priests collected money from horn-shaped containers where Jews deposited the Temple tax and payments for wood, incense, and animal offerings.

A historian from the time, Flavius Josephus, wrote about the traditions of temple life. Jewish men could continue on through brass gates that opened to another set of stairs leading to the Court of the Israelites. Here stood the altar where priests in white linen robes and tubular hats performed sacrificial rituals. Following the instructions in the Book of Exodus, priests slaughtered one-year-old, unblemished lambs or goats. After slitting the animals' throats, they collected the blood, which was considered holy, in silver goblets. Then they splattered the blood on the sides and base of the altar. As they roasted the butchered animals on pomegranate wood, fragrant clouds of smoke drifted over Jerusalem.

Only priests were allowed inside the Temple itself. A curtain, embroidered with a map of the known world, shielded this area from view. Another curtain concealed the innermost room, the Holy of Holies. Only the high priest could enter this room, and only on the Day of Atonement—when God was asked to forgive all sins. Inside this room was a stone on the spot where the Ark of the Covenant would have stood—it had been lost centuries earlier.

The Temple in Jesus' time stood on the site of the first Temple, built by KING SOLOMON many centuries earlier. IN 35 B.C.E., Herod built a fortress into the northern wall of the Temple to protect against enemy invasions from the north.

Archaeologists have been excavating tunnels like this one beneath the Temple's Western Wall since the 1900s C.E. to uncover what the structure was like during the time of Jesus.

DID YOU KNOW?

The Jews generally AVOIDED the SAMARITANS. The Samaritans claimed to be descendants of the Israelites just like the Jews, but the Jews believed the Samaritans were NOT TRUE JEWS because they had intermarried with the Jews' ASSYRIAN ENEMIES. A Samaritan helping a Jew—or vice versa—was unheard of. This parable told people to overcome their prejudices and TO HELP ONE ANOTHER.

"The Good Samaritan," by Giuseppe Zannoni (1850–1899), date unknown

LUKE 10:25–37

THE GOOD SAMARITAN

One day, a student asked Jesus, "What must I do to inherit eternal life?"

Jesus answered, "What is written in the law?"

The student recited phrases from the Old Testament: "Love the Lord your God with all your heart and with all your soul . . . and love your neighbor as yourself."

Jesus told the student that if he did those things he would inherit eternal life.

But the student wanted to show that he was an expert, so he asked Jesus, "Who is my neighbor?"

Instead of answering the question, Jesus told the following story.

One day, a Jewish traveler was going from Jerusalem to Jericho. The road was dangerous. Towns were few and far between, and the rocky terrain provided places for thieves to hide in wait for unsuspecting travelers.

Robbers attacked the man and beat him until he was unconscious. Then they took his clothes and left him for dead.

Not long after, a Jewish priest traveling the same road spotted the wounded man up ahead. But instead of helping the wounded man, the priest crossed the road and hurried along on the opposite side.

A second traveler did the same.

The third traveler, who was a Samaritan, saw the wounded man and felt sorry for him. Although Samaritans were usually enemies of the Jews, he stopped, treated the man's wounds, and bandaged him. Gently, the Samaritan helped the man onto the Samaritan's own donkey and brought him to the nearest inn.

Before leaving the inn, the Samaritan gave the innkeeper enough money to pay for the man's stay.

When Jesus finished telling the story, he asked the student, "Who do you think was a neighbor to the injured man?"

The student answered, "The one who showed mercy."

Jesus told the student, "Go and do likewise."

TEL MEGIDDO: THE TRUE ARMAGEDDON?

Some archaeological sites are known for lavish palaces, others for the artifacts taken from their graves. Tel Megiddo, about 18 miles (29 km) from present-day Haifa, is known for war. The ancient fortified city here was the site of more battles than anywhere else in the biblical world—largely because of its central location.

Megiddo guarded an ancient trade route, the Via Maris (Way of the Sea), which connected Egypt to Syria and Mesopotamia. It also stood watch over roads that branched off this main route and led to major cities such as Jerusalem and Hebron. Megiddo was liked because of its dependable freshwater springs, where travelers stopped before entering the desert. These treasured waters are mentioned in the Song of Deborah in the Bible's Book of Judges.

Outside of the Bible, Megiddo is noted in an account of the Egyptian pharaoh Thutmose III's invasion of the city in 1479 B.C.E. Thutmose III considered Megiddo's central position so important that he inscribed on the Temple at Karnak these words: "The capture of Megiddo is [worth] the capture of a thousand towns."

St. John has a vision of Armageddon in this detail from an altarpiece by Hans Burgkmair the Elder.

Archaeologists digging at Megiddo have uncovered at least 20 layers of settlements: Each one was built on the ruins of the settlement that came before it. The city was inhabited from about 7000 to 500 B.C.E. Later, Megiddo became a fortified city-state. As Megiddo grew in wealth and importance, massive walls were built along with a six-chambered gate, providing levels of protection for a city built for war.

Even Megiddo's water system was built with war in mind. In case of a siege, when the city might be surrounded by an enemy who would cut off the food and water supply, a secret underground passageway led to a spring outside the city walls. Townspeople would descend 183 stairs and walk through a 200-foot (61-m)-long tunnel unknown to the enemy.

One of the many exciting finds among Megiddo's extraordinary temples, palaces, and waterworks were stables, which may date back to the ninth century B.C.E. and have been built by King Ahab. Long, parallel corridors within the stables are believed to have once housed as many as 450 horses.

As if Megiddo's history of bloodshed wasn't enough, John in the Book of Revelation indicates there is at least one more battle in Megiddo's future: the battle to end all battles—Armageddon. Many Bible experts believe that the place named Har Megiddo, which means "hill of Megiddo," gradually came to be called Armageddon. It is here, the Bible prophesies, that forces will gather at the end of the world for one last war pitting good against evil.

In the Bible, **TWO KINGS OF JUDAH, Ahaziah and Josiah,** died on the battlefield at **Megiddo.** Ahaziah was killed by Jehu, King of Israel, and Josiah by Pharaoh Neco of Egypt. Their bodies were **taken to Jerusalem to be buried.**

ruins of the defensive walls for the settlement on the hill that was once the important city-state of Megiddo

THE HOUSE OF PETER

The Book of Matthew tells us that Jesus lived in a fishing village called Capernaum, on the Sea of Galilee. He began his ministry there, teaching in the village synagogue. According to the Gospels, this is where Jesus became known for healing the sick and recruited his first disciples. Among them was Simon, whom Jesus renamed Peter. Today the well-preserved remains of Capernaum's synagogue attract Christian pilgrims to the site where Jesus may have first taught. Not far from the synagogue may have been the house where Peter and Jesus lived.

Archaeologists working in Capernaum on an eight-sided Byzantine church found a small home beneath the rubble. The house dates to the first century B.C.E. Several small rooms surrounded two open courtyards. The walls were made from stone and the roofs of earth and straw. What surprised the experts were the changes made to the house in the middle of the first century C.E. Shortly after the time of Jesus' death, the walls of the main room were covered with a mixture called plaster to hide the stone. The contents of the house changed, too. It had once been stocked with cooking pots and bowls, but the renovated structure contained large storage jars and oil lamps. Experts realized that the purpose of the house had changed. It went from being a private home to being a public meeting place, possibly one of the earliest Christian gathering spots.

In the painting "St. Peter Penitent" by Guercino, 1639 C.E., Peter asks for God's forgiveness.

Over the next few centuries, other renovations were made. The room that had been plastered in the first renovation was turned into the main hall of a church. A stone roof was installed, supported by a two-story arch. Fresh plaster was applied to the old stone walls and painted. Scratched into the plaster were sketches of crosses and a boat. There were also inscriptions relating to Jesus, such as "Lord Jesus Christ help thy servant" and "Christ have mercy." These have helped experts understand the earliest days of Christianity.

Archaeologists still debate whether or not the name Peter appears in the inscriptions. But they've found other clues that could point to Peter: Several fishhooks were discovered, meaning someone had been fishing. Could the hooks have belonged to the fisherman Peter or his brother? Could this have been Peter's house? Many believe so and call it the House of Peter. In the fifth century C.E., an octagonal martyrium church was built in the place of the earlier and simpler church. Octagonal, or eight-sided, objects were symbols of resurrection. This comes from the Bible account that Jesus rose from the dead eight days after entering Jerusalem. A martyrium is built to honor an important event related to Jesus or to shelter the tomb of a martyr. Many served as churches, too.

A **MARTYRIUM** that survives today in Jerusalem is the **Church of the Holy Sepulchre.** Honoring Jesus, it is **BUILT ABOVE THE AREA** where it is believed he was crucified, buried, and resurrected.

ruins of the ancient synagogue in Capernaum, on the northern shore of the Sea of Galilee

DID YOU KNOW?

GOLGOTHA, OR THE "PLACE OF THE SKULL," as described in the Gospels, was **a skull-shaped hill** that once stood outside Jerusalem. Christian tradition says that **JESUS WAS CRUCIFIED HERE.** Today, the spot is marked by **the Church of the Holy Sepulchre.** Upon entering the church, visitors can see **THE STONE OF ANOINTING, a pink slab on which the body of Jesus was thought to have been prepared for burial.** Nearby is a SHRINE that is believed to contain **JESUS' TOMB.** The church was originally built in the fourth century C.E. by the Roman Emperor **Constantine.** During construction, **HIS MOTHER, HELENA,** is said to have located the tomb.

"The Appearance of Christ to Mary Magdalene," by Alexander Andreyevich Ivanov, 1835 C.E.

MARY MAGDALENE AND JESUS' EMPTY TOMB

Joseph of Arimathea, a wealthy Jewish councilman, was a secret disciple of Jesus. When he found out that Jesus was to be buried like a common criminal, he boldly appealed to the governor, Pontius Pilate, to let him have Jesus' body. Pilate agreed.

Joseph and another wealthy follower, Nicodemus, carried Jesus' body from the Crucifixion site. They anointed him with spices worthy of a king, wrapped him in linen cloths, and buried him in the tomb that Joseph had created for his own burial—a cavelike hole cut in a hillside. Before the sun set on the Sabbath, they rolled a large stone against the tomb's opening.

Mary Magdalene and Mary the mother of James and Joseph were among Jesus' followers who had stayed with him as he suffered on the cross. Now they watched as the men blocked the tomb.

The next morning, as the sun rose, the two Marys carried more spices to the tomb to again anoint Jesus' body. They likely wondered how they would roll away the stone.

As they arrived at the tomb, the earth began to shake. An angel dressed in white rolled the giant stone away. He told the women, "Don't be afraid. I know you are looking for Jesus. Jesus is not here. He has been raised from the dead. Go tell Peter and the others that Jesus will be at Galilee, just as he said he would."

Mary Magdalene and Mary were frightened but also filled with joy that Jesus had risen. They were running from the tomb to find the disciples when suddenly they heard, "Greetings." It was Jesus. Mary Magdalene and Mary dropped to the ground and took hold of his feet. "Do not be afraid," Jesus said. "Go and tell my brothers to go to Galilee; there they will see me."

ACTS 9

CONVERSION OF PAUL

Saul was a Jewish tentmaker who took a stand against Jews who joined the Christian movement. He set out for the city of Damascus with a group of men to hunt them down. As they neared Damascus, a blinding light flashed from the sky. Saul heard a voice say, “Why do you persecute me?”

Saul asked, “Who are you?”

“I am Jesus whom you are persecuting.” Jesus then told Saul to go to Damascus, where he would receive further instructions.

Saul scrambled to his feet only to discover that, although his eyes were wide open, he could not see. The brilliant light had blinded him.

For three days Saul remained blind. He neither ate nor drank, waiting for instructions from God.

Meanwhile, a follower of Jesus named Ananias also had a vision. In the vision, the Lord told Ananias to lay his hands on Saul to cure his blindness. Ananias was surprised by the Lord’s command. He had heard ugly reports about the way Saul treated Jesus’ followers. Why would the Lord choose to heal this man?

The Lord explained his plans for Saul: “He is an instrument whom I have chosen to bring my name before Gentiles and kings and before the people of Israel.”

Ananias did as the Lord commanded. He went to the house where Saul was waiting and laid his hands on Saul. The moment Ananias touched him, scales fell from Saul’s eyes and he could see. He promised to spread the word of Jesus for the rest of his life.

To show his newfound devotion to Jesus, Saul was baptized and given the name we know today: Paul. Paul set out on missionary journeys, bringing many followers to Christianity. This came at a heavy cost, from physical beatings to years in prison. But nothing kept Paul from his faith.

“The Conversion of St. Paul,” by Bartholomeus Spranger, about 1572 C.E.

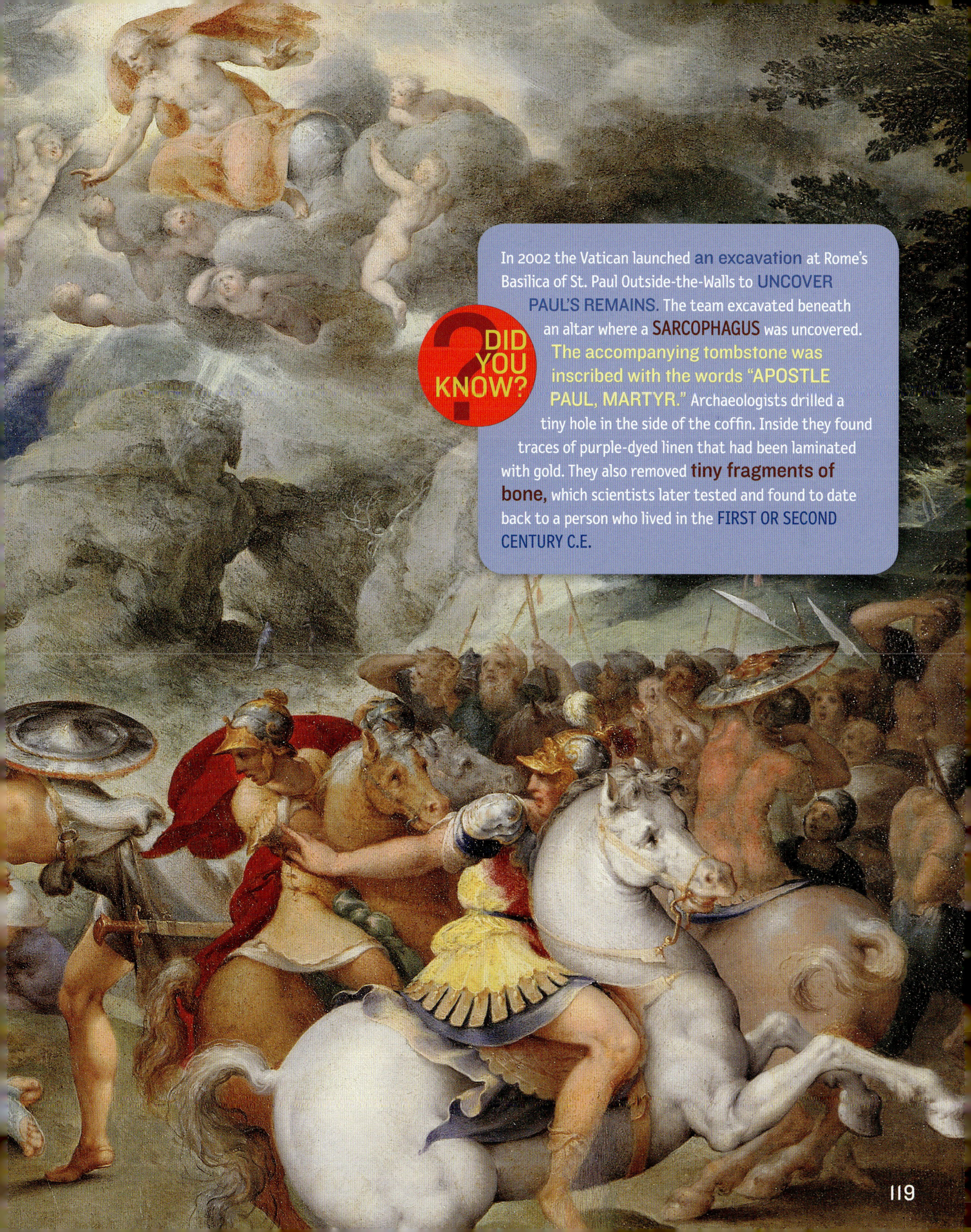

DID YOU KNOW?

In 2002 the Vatican launched **an excavation** at Rome's Basilica of St. Paul Outside-the-Walls to **UNCOVER PAUL'S REMAINS.** The team excavated beneath an altar where a **SARCOPHAGUS** was uncovered. **The accompanying tombstone was inscribed with the words "APOSTLE PAUL, MARTYR."** Archaeologists drilled a tiny hole in the side of the coffin. Inside they found traces of purple-dyed linen that had been laminated with gold. They also removed **tiny fragments of bone,** which scientists later tested and found to date back to a person who lived in the **FIRST OR SECOND CENTURY C.E.**

These niche graves in Rome's Catacombs of St. Callixtus were burial places for many Christian martyrs and leaders.

SECRETS OF THE ROMAN CATACOMBS

During the early days of Christianity, burying the dead within Rome's city walls was forbidden by law. Because Christians in Rome wished to bury their dead instead of following the Roman custom of burning, or cremation, they had to find another way. They began digging into the volcanic rock below the city to create an underground cemetery, or catacomb. Over time they dug vast networks of underground tunnels.

Into the tunnel walls they carved rectangular burial niches where the bodies of loved ones, wrapped in linen, were laid to rest. Families sealed these niche graves with a slab of marble if they could afford it, or baked clay if not. The name of the deceased, and often symbols, were carved into these grave covers.

Catacomb symbols include the fish, meaning Christ, and the anchor, meaning safety.

Although the disciple Paul was likely buried outside the city in a family tomb after his death around 65 C.E., it is believed that his remains were hidden in the catacombs during a time of unrest between 69 and 79 C.E.

At the end of the eighth and the beginning of the ninth centuries, Rome's enemies toppled monuments and stole objects from holy places, including the catacombs. Under the direction of the popes, the relics, or remains, of martyrs and saints were removed and hidden for safekeeping. Once emptied, the catacombs were forgotten. The entrances filled in and grew over.

At the turn of the 16th century, the catacombs captured the interest of an Italian lawyer, Antonio Bosio. His extensive explorations of the underground labyrinths earned him the nickname "Christopher Columbus of the Catacombs." Back then, archaeology was more about taking treasures for wealthy patrons than investigating the past and recording those finds. Bosio, however, turned archaeology into a science. He hired artists to accurately copy the frescoes, mosaics, and other artwork he discovered in the catacombs. He surveyed the confusing maze of passageways and made careful records.

Many of the symbols that Bosio discovered date back to the early days of Christianity when Christians were considered villains. For fear of being persecuted, Christians used symbols to express their faith to one another. The dove carrying an olive branch symbolized peace. The anchor symbolized safety and security for the soul in the next life. And the phoenix, a mythical bird that rose from the ashes, symbolized resurrection of the dead. The fish symbol stood for Christ.

Nearly 2,000 years after his death, in 2002, a tomb bearing Paul's name was uncovered beneath the altar in the Basilica of St. Paul Outside-the-Walls, named for its place on the outskirts of Rome's main city. Archaeologist Giorgio Filippi at Rome's Vatican Museums said that the tomb is on the site traditionally believed to be Paul's first tomb. Perhaps Paul's remains stayed in one place for two centuries. But a possible brief time hidden in the catacombs may have saved them from destruction.

The CATACOMB PASSAGEWAYS were confusing **mazes that covered nearly 600 ACRES** (2.5 sq km), connecting galleries and chambers. Visitors climbed down FOUR STORIES OF NARROW STAIRS to reach them.

GLOSSARY

admonition A warning

Akkadian An ancient language of the Sumerians, people of Sumer

amphora A clay jar that held oil and wine

ancestor A person in someone's family from an earlier time

apostle One who is sent out to spread the word of God. The Twelve Apostles were the main disciples, or students, of Jesus.

aqueduct A Roman-made bridge that carried water above-ground

Aramaeans An ancient people who came from Syria. They spoke Aramaic.

Aramaic One of the first languages of the written Bible. Jesus probably spoke it.

archaeologist Someone who studies the history of the earliest people by examining tools, bones, and other items left behind

Ark of the Covenant A chest containing the tablets on which the Ten Commandments were written

Assyrians An ancient people of Mesopotamia, who defeated the northern kingdom of Israel in 722 B.C.E.

atonement Apologizing for doing something wrong and promising to be better

Babylonians An ancient people from central-southern Mesopotamia, who besieged Jerusalem and began to exile the Jews in 597 B.C.E.

B.C.E. Meaning "before the Common Era," it is usually used for dates before the birth of Christ.

birthright Special privileges given to the oldest child

bitumen Black tarry substance used for building

books of the Bible The major sections that make up the Bible, often named after events, peoples, prophets, kings, or apostles

bulrushes Large grasses that grow at the edge of a wetland

Canaanites Citizens of Canaan, in the area of today's Israel, where Moses took the Israelites after leaving Egypt

carbon dating A method for determining the age of ancient carbon-bearing objects, including mummies and fossils, by measuring the level of decay in their carbon

catacombs Underground passageways where early Christians worshipped and buried their dead

C.E. Meaning "Common Era" and generally used for dates after the birth of Christ

census The official counting of the number of people in a country

chariot A carriage pulled by horses and used by warriors in early battles

cherub A heavenly being. One guarded the gate to Eden after Adam and Eve were turned out.

city-state A city-size state with its own government

cuneiform Early writing using wedge-shaped instruments

curator A museum expert who manages a collection of objects

deathbed blessing Blessing given to the oldest son by a father who is about to die

descendant Someone who has come from a particular family

disciple A follower of Jesus. The 12 main disciples chosen to spread Jesus' message were called apostles.

Dome of the Rock A Muslim shrine built over the site of Solomon's Temple

dowry Payment to the groom by the bride's family

embalm To artificially preserve a body before burial

exile A period during which a person is forced to live away from home

exodus A situation in which many people leave their home at the same time; for instance, the Israelites made an exodus from Egypt.

Fertile Crescent A crescent-shaped region of farmland stretching from ancient Egypt to Mesopotamia (mostly today's Iraq)

generation The average length of time between the birth of parents and the birth of their children

Gospels The first four books of the New Testament

Herodium The palace-fortress of King Herod, outside Jerusalem

Hittites Ancient people of Anatolia (today's Turkey) and neighbors of Israel since the time of Abraham

idol An image of a false god

incense A pleasant-smelling substance often burned in religious ceremonies

inscribed Written into or carved into

javelin A light spear usually used as a weapon in ancient wars (also new)

Judah The new kingdom created when Israel was divided into two after Solomon's death

judge In the Bible, a decision-maker in a court of law and also a military leader

ketubah A system protecting the personal money of a husband or wife

Law of Moses The Torah, or first five books of the Hebrew Bible, believed to have been written by Moses

manna Honeyed wafers God sent to feed Moses and the Israelites in the desert

martyrium A building that honors either Jesus or a martyr

Mesopotamia Considered the Western world's earliest civilization, it was made up of mostly today's Iraq and also parts of Kuwait, Syria, Turkey, and Iran.

Messiah A name given to Jesus as a prophet

midwife A woman who helps deliver babies

ministry Bringing religious teachings to people

miracle A surprising event that can't be explained by natural or scientific laws and attributed to God's work

Nebuchadnezzar Babylonian king who destroyed the Temple of Jerusalem and sent the Jews into exile

Nile Delta Area where the Nile River empties into the Mediterranean Sea

Nineveh Capital of ancient Assyria, built by King Sennacherib

oasis An area in the desert with a water source, where plants grow

offering Something that is given to God as a gift

ostracon A potsherd with writing on it

papyrus A grassy marsh plant used for making paperlike material

parable A simple story to teach a lesson

patriarch The oldest male head of the family

pharaoh A ruler of ancient Egypt

Philistines An ancient people who lived along the Mediterranean Coast near Israel; archenemies of Israel

Phoenicians An ancient seafaring people who served as traders

plaster A wet substance that hardens when dry and is used to smooth walls

potsherd Piece of ancient pottery found at an archaeological site

prodigal Wasteful

Promised Land The land God promised to the descendants of Abraham. Once called Canaan, it lay on the Mediterranean Sea between the river of Egypt and the Euphrates River, near today's Israel.

prophet Someone who delivers messages, omens, or warnings that are believed to come from God

relief A sculpture carved into a wall

replica An exact copy of an object, usually in a smaller size resurrection The rising of Christ from the dead

resurrection The rising of Christ from the dead

Romans Citizens of ancient Rome; they occupied much of the Mediterranean Coast.

Sabbath The day of rest and worship, as God intended; among the Jews it is celebrated from Friday evening to Saturday evening.

Samaritan A stranger from Samaria, shunned by the people of Israel; today it means one who helps a person in need.

sarcophagus An ancient stone coffin

scroll Rolled up paper or leather or parchment, made from sheepskin or goatskin, with writing on it

submersible A submarine archaeologists use to study ancient shipwrecks

Sumer The first civilization in Mesopotamia with a complex city; residents were called Sumerians.

synagogue A building used for Jewish religious services

tell (or tel) A hill created by many generations of people living and building in one spot

Temple currency Special coins used for temple purchases, with no images of humans or animals.

Temple Mount The site in Jerusalem where Solomon's Temple was built

tsunami Massive wave caused by an underwater earthquake

wadi A dry riverbed that fills with water only during rain

ziggurat A massive templelike structure built in ancient Mesopotamia

PERSONALITIES

It's hard to pick just a few personalities from the thousands of larger-than-life heroes and villains, kings and workers, leaders and lost souls who fill the Bible. Here are just a few of the extraordinary men and women in the Bible.

Name: Abraham

Vitals: Introduced in the Book of Genesis; the first patriarch, or forefather, of the Israelites

Famous for: Being so devoted to God as a simple shepherd that he was rewarded with descendants as "numerous as the stars of heaven." This "father of many" gave rise to three of the world's great religions—Judaism, Christianity, and Islam.

Name: Moses

Vitals: Introduced in Genesis. Born a Hebrew, he was adopted by Pharaoh's daughter and grew up as an Egyptian noble.

Famous for: Freeing the Jews from slavery, leading them out of Egypt, guiding them through the desert for 40 years to the Promised Land, and receiving the Ten Commandments from God at Mount Sinai

Name: David

Vitals: Introduced in the first Book of Samuel, he was the youngest son of Jesse, and a great warrior.

Famous for: Knocking down the giant Goliath with a single stone from his slingshot. David later became king, replacing Saul, who disobeyed God. Despite jealousy and plots of murder against him, David united Israel's 12 tribes into a single nation.

Name: Deborah

Vitals: The only female judge of the Israelites mentioned in the Bible. She was also a prophet and a warrior.

Famous for: Successfully leading the Israelites in battle against Jabin, King of Canaan. The Song of Deborah tells of the heroism of Deborah and another strong woman, Jael.

Name: Solomon

Vitals: Introduced in the second Book of Samuel, Solomon was David and Bathsheba's son.

Famous for: His legendary wisdom, a gift from God. He became king after David, instead of his older brothers, and later built the First Temple to God in Jerusalem. He ended in ruin when he turned to other gods.

FROM THE BIBLE

Name: Jesus

Vitals: Introduced by name in the New Testament: Matthew 1:1. The son of God, born to Mary and Joseph. The four Gospels follow his life.

Famous for: Being the central figure of Christianity as its long-awaited savior, dying on the Cross for humankind's sins, and rising from the dead. His teachings of compassion and forgiveness fill the New Testament.

Name: Mary

Vitals: Introduced by name in the Books of Matthew and Luke when the angel Gabriel told her she would be the mother of the Messiah, or Jesus

Famous for: Being the mother of Jesus. Mary raised Jesus and became his follower, and then she stayed at the foot of the Cross as he died. For Christians, Mary has become the most revered woman in the Bible.

Name: Paul (Roman name), formerly Saul (Jewish name)

Vitals: Introduced in Acts as Saul of Tarsus, a tentmaker. He was committed to mistreating anyone who became a Christian.

Famous for: Becoming a Christian when Jesus appeared to him in a bolt of lightning on the road to Damascus. Using the name Paul, his Roman name, he spread Christianity to new lands. His writings help make up the New Testament.

Name: The Apostles—the original 12 were Simon Peter, James, John, Andrew, Philip, Thomas, Bartholomew, Matthew, James (the Lesser), Simon, Thaddaeus, and Judas Iscariot.

Vitals: Introduced in Matthew, these 12 followers of Jesus were early Christian missionaries, healers, and leaders.

Famous for: Being chosen by Jesus to spread his message. They were given power to cast out evil spirits and heal the sick. Jesus warned that many people would be against them: "I am sending you out like sheep in the midst of wolves . . ."

Name: John the Baptist

Vitals: In Luke, the angel Gabriel told John's elderly father that he and his wife would have a son who would pave the way for the Messiah.

Famous for: Preaching the coming of Jesus, and later baptizing him. John had a large following in the Wilderness of Judea, where he baptized people for the forgiveness of sins. King Herod beheaded John for speaking out against him.

Name: Mary Magdalene

Vitals: Introduced in Matthew as witness to Jesus' Crucifixion. Later, in Luke, her story is told from the beginning, when she first met Jesus.

Famous for: Witnessing Jesus' Crucifixion, discovering his empty tomb, and being the first to see him after his resurrection. Mary Magdalene was one of Jesus' followers, who traveled with him during his days of teaching.

INDEX

Boldface indicates illustrations.

RESOURCES

To learn more about the people, places, events, and archaeology of the biblical world, look into these sources:

Books

Bowker, John. *The Complete Bible Handbook*. DK Publishing, 2001.

Cline, Eric. *From Eden to Exile: Unraveling Mysteries of the Bible*. National Geographic, 2008.

Collins, Michael, editor. *The Illustrated Bible Story by Story*. DK Publishing, 2012.

Currie, Robin, and Stephen Hyslop. *The Letter and the Scroll: What Archaeology Tells Us About the Bible*. National Geographic, 2009.

Dersin, Denise. *What Life Was Like on the Banks of the Nile*. Time Life Education, 1997.

Esposito, John, and Susan Tyler Hitchcock. *Geography of Religion*. National Geographic, 2006.

Fischer, Jean, and Tracy M. Sumner. *Big Bible Guide: Kids' Bible Dictionary & Handbook*. Barbour Publishing, Inc., 2013.

Geoghegan, Jeffrey, and Michael Homan. *The Bible for Dummies*. John Wiley & Sons, Inc., 2003.

Isbouts, Jean-Pierre. *The Biblical World: An Illustrated Atlas*. National Geographic, 2007.

———. *Who's Who in the Bible: Unforgettable People and Timeless Stories From Genesis to Revelation*. National Geographic, 2013.

Lloyd-Jones, Sally. *The Jesus Storybook Bible*. Zondervan Publishing, 2007.

Miller, Stephen M. *The Complete Guide to the Bible*. Barbour Publishing, Inc., 2007.

Schneider, Tammi J. *Mothers of Promise: Women in the Book of Genesis*. Baker Academic, 2008.

Websites

biblegateway.com (NRSV)*
bible-history.com
biblehub.com
bible.org
bibleplaces.com
bibleresources.americanbible.org
biblicalarchaeology.org
jewishvirtuallibrary.org
thekingsbible.com
oxfordbiblicalstudies.com
studylight.org

CREDITS

Front cover: (tower), Wikimedia Commons; (cross), Christopher Hall/Shutterstock; (archeologist), Michael Melford/NG Creative; (well), albund/Shutterstock; (apple), Mega Pixel/Shutterstock; (wheat), marilyn barbone/Shutterstock; (lamb), JMichl/Shutterstock; (apostles), Renata Sedmakova/Shutterstock; (palm), COLOA Studio/Shutterstock; (ark), Noah's Ark frieze at Chiesa di San Maurizio al Monastero Maggiore/Bailey-Cooper Photography/Alamy Stock Photo; **back cover:** (Bible), vipman/Shutterstock; (Masada ruins), Cosmo Condina Middle East/Alamy Stock Photo; (tablet), Rolf Marriott/NG Creative; (lion), Eric Isselée/Shutterstock; **spine:** thaagoon/Shutterstock; 1, George Dukinas/Shutterstock; 3 (UP LE), albund/Shutterstock; 3 (UP RT), Mega Pixel/Shutterstock; 3 (LO LE), Marilyn Barbone/Shutterstock; 3 (LO RT), JMichl/E+/Getty Images; 4–5 (Background), eFesenko/Shutterstock; 4 (UP), St. Peter by Guercino (Giovanni Francesco Barbieri) (1591–1666), Palazzo Venezia, Rome, Italy/Bridgeman Images; 4 (LO), Painting by Carl Bloch/Hulton Fine Art Collection/Photo by Rischgitz/Getty Images; 5 (LE), photostockam/Shutterstock; 5 (RT), Mary Evans Picture Library/Alamy Stock Photo; 6, The Conversion of St. Paul painting of Marco da Siena (1545) in church Santo Spirito in Sassia/Renata Sedmakova/Shutterstock; 8 (UP RT), DEA/Veneranda Biblioteca Ambrosiana/De Agostini/Getty Images; 8 (CTR LE) David Soanes/Shutterstock; 8 (LO LE), Robert Clark/National Geographic Creative; 8 (LO RT), Heritage Images/Corbis; 8 (LO CTR), Moses presenting the Ten Commandments (fresco), Raphael (Raffaello Sanzio of Urbino) (1483–1520)/Basilica di San Pietro, Rome, Italy/Bridgeman Images; 9 (UP LE), Zvonimir Atletic/Shutterstock; 9 (UP CTR), The Gallery Collection/Corbis; 9 (CTR LE), Rolf Marriott/National Geographic Creative; 9 (CTR), David and Goliath, illustration from 'Bible Stories', 1968 (colour litho), D'Achille, Gino (20th century)/Private Collection/Bridgeman Images; 9 (CTR RT), Wikimedia Commons ; 9 (LO LE), The Child Jesus Disputing in the Temple, c.1545 (oil on canvas), Bordone, Paris (1500–71)/Isabella Stewart Gardner Museum, Boston, MA, USA/Bridgeman Images; 9 (LO RT), Michael Nicholson/Corbis; 10–11, The Creation of the Birds and Fishes (oil on copper) (see 307914, 307916), Oosten, Isaak van (1613–61)/Private Collection/Johnny Van Haeften Ltd., London/Bridgeman Images; 12–13, Peter Horree/Alamy Stock Photo; 14, DEA/G. Dagli Orti/Getty Images; 15, mitja2/iStock; 16–17, Fine Art Images/Heritage Images/Getty Images; 18, Underwood and Underwood/National Geographic Creative; 19, Rolf Marriott/National Geographic Creative; 20–21, Wikimedia Commons; 22–23, Renata Sedmakova/Shutterstock; 24–25, Wikimedia Commons; 26, Duby Tal/Albatross/Alamy Stock Photo; 27, Buurserstraat386/Dreamstime; 28–29, Wikimedia Commons; 30–31, Isaac Blessing Jacob, c.1638 (oil on canvas), Flinck, Govaert (1615–60)/Rijksmuseum, Amsterdam, The Netherlands/Bridgeman Images; 32–33, Jacob's Dream (oil on canvas), Rosa, Salvator (1615–73)/Collection of the Duke of Devonshire, Chatsworth House, UK/©Devonshire Collection, Chatsworth/Reproduced by permission of Chatsworth Settlement Trustees/Bridgeman Images; 34, The Gallery Collection/Corbis; 35, Hemis/Alamy Stock Photo; 36–37, Joseph's coat of many colours brought to his father, Jacob, English School, (19th century)/Private Collection/Look and Learn/Bridgeman Images; 38, M. Carrieri/Bridgeman Images; 39, Michael Hampshire/National Geographic Creative; 40–41, Barak and Deborah (oil on canvas) (detail of 67670), Solimena, Francesco (1657–1747)/Private Collection/Bridgeman Images; 42, Winfield Parks/National Geographic Creative; 43, Robert Clark/National Geographic Creative; 44–45, Heritage Images/Corbis; 46, De Agostini/S. Vannini/The Granger Collection; 47 Prisma Bildagentur AG/Alamy Stock Photo; 48–49, Seventh Plague of Egypt, 1823 (oil on canvas), Martin, John (1789–1854)/Museum of Fine Arts, Boston, MA, USA/Francis Welch Fund/Bridgeman Images; 50, Renata Sedmakova/Shutterstock; 51, Jean-Pierre Isbouts; 52–53, Renata Sedmakova/Shutterstock; 54–55, Moses presenting the Ten Commandments (fresco), Raphael (Raffaello Sanzio of Urbino) (1483–1520)/Basilica di San Pietro, Rome, Italy/Bridgeman Images; 56, Hebrew University/Getty Images; 57, Magica/Alamy Stock Photo; 58, Hanan Isachar/Alamy Stock Photo; 59, Lebrecht Music and Arts Photo Library/Alamy Stock Photo; 60–61, Ailsa Mellon Bruce Fund/Wikimedia Commons; 62, Bill McKelvie/Shutterstock; 63, H. Tom Hall/National Geographic Creative; 64–65, Samson Betrayed by Delilah, by Felice Giani, 1784/Galleria Nazionale, Parma, Italy/Mondadori Portfolio/Art Resource, NY; 66, Compiling and editing the canon of Scripture from ancient documents and records, Hole, William Brassey (1846–1917)/Private Collection/Look and Learn/Bridgeman Images; 67, Captmondo/Wikipedia; 68–69, Michael Nicholson/Corbis; 70, Dereje/Shutterstock; 71, Wikimedia Commons; 72–73, David and Goliath, illustration from 'Bible Stories', 1968 (colour litho), D'Achille, Gino (20th century)/Private Collection/Bridgeman Images; 74, Bible Land Pictures/Alamy Stock Photo; 75, Nir Alon/Alamy Stock Photo; 76, Balage Balog/Archaeology Illustrated; 77, 'House of David' inscribed on a victory stele, Tel Dan (basalt), Iron Age (9th Century BC)/The Israel Museum, Jerusalem, Israel/Bridgeman Images; 78–79, The judgment of Solomon, by Francesco Podesti (1800–1895)/De Agostini Picture Library/F. Gallino/Bridgeman Images; 80, Eric Cline; 81, Anton Ivanov/Shutterstock; 82–83, Christie's Images/Corbis; 84, Hanan Isachar/Alamy Stock Photo; 85, Herod and Herodias at the Feast of Herod (oil on panel) (detail of 222483), Francken, Frans the Elder (1542–1616)/Musee Municipal, Dunkirk, France/Bridgeman Images; 86–87, Wikimedia Commons; 88–89, Image courtesy of the National Gallery of Art; 90, DeAgostini/Getty Images; 91, Jozef Sedmak/Alamy Stock Photo; 92–93, The Child Jesus Disputing in the Temple, c.1545 (oil on canvas), Bordone, Paris (1500–71)/Isabella Stewart Gardner Museum, Boston, MA, USA/Bridgeman Images; 94–95, Philadelphia Museum of Art/Corbis; 96–97, The Sermon on the Mount (figures possibly by Hans Jordeans), Momper, Joos or Josse de, The Younger (1564–1635)/Johnny van Haeften Gallery, London, UK/Bridgeman Images; 98, Shai Ginott/Corbis; 99, Pantheon Studios; 100–101, Brooklyn Museum/Corbis; 102–103, The Gallery Collection/Corbis; 104–105, Return of the Prodigal Son (oil on canvas), Palma Il Giovane (Jacopo Negretti) (1548–1628)/Galleria dell' Accademia, Venice, Italy/Cameraphoto Arte Venezia/Bridgeman Images; 106–107, Renata Sedmakova/Shutterstock; 108, Berthold Werner; 109, Menahem Kahana/AFP/Getty Images; 110–111, The Good Samaritan, by Giuseppe Zannoni, 1850–1899, 19th Century, canvas, Italy, Veneto, Verona, Civic Modern Art Gallery/Sergio Anelli/Electa/Mondadori Portfolio/Getty Images; 112, Saint John's vision at Patmos, detail from Saint John altarpiece, 1518, by Hans Burgkmair Elder (1473–1531), Germany, 16th century, Burgkmair, Hans (c.1473–1531)/Alte Pinakothek, Munich, Germany/De Agostini Picture Library/Bridgeman Images; 113, Jean-Pierre Isbouts; 114, St. Peter by Guercino (Giovanni Francesco Barbieri) (1591–1666), Palazzo Venezia, Rome, Italy/Bridgeman Images; 115, Jean-Pierre Isbouts; 116–117, Wikimedia Commons; 118–119, DEA/Veneranda Biblioteca Ambrosiana/De Agostini/Getty Images; 120, David Soanes/Shutterstock; 121, Bible Land Pictures/Alamy Stock Photo; 124 (Abraham), Renata Sedmakova/Shutterstock; 124 (Moses), Mary Evans Picture Library/Alamy Stock Photo; 124 (David), Renata Sedmakova/Shutterstock; 124 (Deborah), Lebrecht Music and Arts Photo Library/Alamy Stock Photo; 124 (Solomon), Chronicle/Alamy Stock Photo; 125 (Jesus), The Good Shepherd, c.1650–60 (oil on canvas), Champaigne, Philippe de (1602–74)/Musee des Beaux-Arts, Tours, France/Bridgeman Images; 125 (Mary), Zvonimir Atletic/Shutterstock; 125 (Saul), Saul is Struck Blind on the Road to Damascus, Dixon, Arthur A. (1872–1959)/Private Collection/Look and Learn/Bridgeman Images; 125 (The Apostles), Renata Sedmakova/Shutterstock; 125 (John the Baptist), Renata Sedmakova/Shutterstock; 125 (Mary Magdalene), Heritage Image Partnership Ltd/Alamy Stock Photo

Since 1888, the National Geographic Society has funded more than 12,000 research, exploration, and preservation projects around the world. The Society receives funds from National Geographic Partners LLC, funded in part by your purchase. A portion of the proceeds from this book supports this vital work. To learn more, visit natgeo.com/info.

NATIONAL GEOGRAPHIC and Yellow Border Design are trademarks of the National Geographic Society, used under license.

For more information, visit nationalgeographic.com, call 1-800-647-5463, or write to the following address:

National Geographic Partners
1145 17th Street N.W.
Washington, D.C. 20036-4688 U.S.A.

Visit us online at
nationalgeographic.com/books

For librarians and teachers:
ngchildrensbooks.org

More for kids from National Geographic:
kids.nationalgeographic.com

For information about special discounts for bulk purchases, please contact National Geographic Books Special Sales: specialsales@natgeo.com

For rights or permissions inquiries, please contact National Geographic Books Subsidiary Rights: bookrights@natgeo.com

Editorial, Design, and Production by Potomac Global Media, LLC

Designed by Carol Farrar Norton

Global Media, LLC, and National Geographic Partners, LLC, would like to thank the following members of the project team: Kevin Mulroy, Barbara Brownell Grogan, Karin Kinney, Kris Hanneman, Jane Sunderland, and Tim Griffin. And from National Geographic Partners: Callie Broaddus and Amanda Larsen, art directors; Angela Modany, associate editor; and Lori Epstein, photo director.

Hardcover ISBN: 978-1-4263-2881-7
Reinforced library binding:
978-1-4263-2882-4

Printed in Hong Kong
17/THK/1